END OF THE RETIREMENT AGE

Embracing the pursuit of meaning, purpose and prosperity

DAVID KENNEDY

First published in 2017 by Grammar Factory Pty Ltd

National Library of Australia Cataloguing-in-Publication entry:

Creator: Kennedy David J. 1978- author.
Title: End of the retirement age / David Kennedy.

ISBN: 9780995445390 (paperback)
9780648137108 (ebook)

> Subjects: Retirement--Australia--Planning.
> Retirement age--Australia.
> Older people--Australia.

Printed in Australia by McPhersons Printing
Cover design by Designerbility
Book production and editorial services by Grammar Factory

General advice warning and disclaimer

*For Kate – an endless source of energy and inspiration;
and Rosie, Fletcher and Sam – let's go to the park.*

CONTENTS

PART 4: PLANNING FOR YOUR FINANCIAL FUTURE IN A WORLD OBSESSED WITH 'NOW'

PART 5: INSPIRING STORIES AS A GENERATION REDEFINES RETIREMENT

FOREWORD

*'They will remain productive for longer,
not just because they need to but because they want
to and because they can.'*

SACHA NAUTA, THE ECONOMIST

What factors contribute to the achievement of success in any venture? The Mona Lisa is regarded as a masterpiece because of the dedicated work and artistic talent of the genius, Leonardo da Vinci. Yet the painting wasn't always as famous, and it didn't always hang in the Louvre.

Beyond the art world, widespread public appreciation of the Mona Lisa only came about after 1911, following the painting's theft, disappearance and mysterious return some years later. The notoriety of the heist surely played a part in creating an aura around the portrait that survives to this day.

We could attribute this chance occurrence to the 'luck factor', and perhaps this means success has three inputs - hard work, talent and luck.

Roman philosopher, Seneca, once said that luck is what happens when preparation meets opportunity - in other words, we make our own luck.

In my experience, you can make your own luck in retirement by focusing on the following:

- Expanding your network of connections.

- Being curious and aware of possibilities that may be good for you.

- Experimenting with new experiences and taking risks.

Who knows, you may meet interesting people, discover further meaning in your life and altogether have fun!

I come from an investment background, and now that I am in semi-retirement, I have had a chance to understand more about the non-financial aspects of life beyond sixty. Our society has placed great emphasis on retirement income and security by introducing the compulsory superannuation system. This is a good thing. However, my recent experience has convinced me that, for some people, the non-financial aspects of retired life, and the pursuit of meaning, can be even more important. Meaning is highly personal - even hard to define - and merits a lot of emotional effort by the individual to come to understand it better.

This handbook to retirement comes at a critical time as more and more retired, or soon-to-be-retired, Australians wrestle with these non-financial considerations.

I was honoured by the offer to contribute to this book. I am impressed by its strength of mission, the quality of writing and the breadth and depth of topics covered.

This is a book full of insight, reflection and advice and should be read from cover to cover. It traverses a broad swathe of territory from matters of public policy to those of individual choice and reflection. It should occupy a place on every older person's bookshelf as a guide to the topic of retirement, that is only now emerging as critical in our society.

There is a very useful section in Part 4 called Practical Steps Towards a Better Retirement, which deserves to be the subject of discussion and debate at many family dinner tables and beyond.

I would recommend this book to everyone over the age of 55, to read and absorb. After all, we all retire at some time. Be prepared!

DR JON GLASS, PHD
DIRECTOR - 64 PLUS

INTRODUCTION

THE END OF THE RETIREMENT AGE

'Musicians don't retire; they stop when there's no more music in them.'

LOUIS ARMSTRONG

We have reached the end of the retirement age.

It is May 2017 and Oxford University Professor of Gerontology, Sarah Harper, is on stage at the annual Hay Festival of Literature and the Arts in Wales, speaking about longer life expectancies and how we might re-imagine a world where more and more people live into their nineties and beyond. She relays a colleague's forecast that around half of the babies born in the UK today will live to age 104, before urging the audience to completely rethink the milestones we reach along life's journey.

'We really are talking about extending lives in a way that I think we've never experienced before,' Harper says. 'And we have to start asking ourselves questions about the sort of world we're going to live in with these very, very long lives. Are we really going to have – this is education, this is work, oh, and this is 50 years retirement? I don't think so … I think it's far more likely that we're going to have far more fluid lives.'

Coined in the 16th century, the word 'retire' is derived from the French 'retirer', which means to withdraw to a place of safety or seclusion.

But that narrative has changed. Retirement, as we know it, has really only been around for a little over 100 years. Today, mature-age

Australians (in their 50s, 60s and 70s) are healthier than ever, living longer than at any other point in history, and have a tremendous amount to offer their communities and the Australian economy.

This book is an optimistic exploration of the forces shaping the evolving retirement landscape, the surprising economic opportunity of an ageing population (if we have the courage to pursue it), and the inspiring ways a generation is redefining retirement.

Due to four converging realities, retirement as we know it is rapidly becoming redundant. The combination of longer life expectancies, declining government capacity to support us as generously as we age, a reduction in job security, and the challenges many face in funding a multi-decade retirement income, mean we need to completely re-think our approach to this phase of life, while taking a fresh look at the challenges and opportunities of an ageing population.

In its simplest form, retirement is a social structure that has failed to evolve. In his book *Thank You for Being Late*, Pulitzer Prize-winning journalist and author Thomas Friedman explores three accelerating forces shaping the world – globalisation, technology and climate change. Friedman refers to Craig Mundie, a supercomputer designer, and former chief of strategy and research at Microsoft, who states, 'when the rate of change eventually exceeds the ability to adapt you get "dislocation". "Disruption" is what happens when someone does something clever that makes you or your company obsolete. "Dislocation" is when the whole environment is being altered so quickly that everyone starts to feel they can't keep up.'

'This is what is happening now,' writes Friedman.

We are fortunate that over time, societies tend to adapt (albeit slowly), and this means a new version of retirement is gradually emerging – one that I will argue is far superior to the original.

The debate about the economic challenges of an ageing population often overlooks the emerging behaviour and preferences of an older generation that is busily redesigning retirement – on their terms. This is a productive generation that is working longer, working more flexibly, embracing technology, and starting businesses in record numbers. Many are determined to continue making a contribution to the community, and it is my contention that an ageing population, which is healthier and living longer than at any other point in history, represents the single greatest economic opportunity of our time. But we must be brave enough to recognise the opportunity in front of us and to seize it with both hands.

We have a choice to make, and now – more than ever – the path we choose matters.

So what happened and why is the retirement age over? Let's start from the beginning.

When the Deakin government passed the Invalid and Old-Age Pensions Act in 1908, the Age Pension was introduced. Men became eligible at 65 and women at age 60, with additional eligibility criteria based on things like character, race and your financial position. The idea was that the state had a moral obligation to look after the financial security of the elderly, who had dutifully paid taxes throughout their working lives.

In 1908, the average life expectancy at birth for males was 55, while women were expected to live to age 59. Given the pension didn't kick in until age 65 for men and 60 for women, from the government's perspective, it was a conveniently designed system that didn't place too much strain on the nation's finances. Only around four per cent of the Australian male population was over 65 in 1908, compared to 14 per cent today. (According to the Australian Bureau of Statistics, this figure is expected to rise to around 25 per cent by 2050.)

More than a century after the Age Pension was introduced, the age of eligibility has barely moved, yet average life expectancy has increased by around 25 years. The possibility of a multi-decade retirement was unfathomable in the early 20th century, as the average male lived into their 50s or 60s. Prior to this point, you were less likely to retire and more likely to work until you dropped dead.

As the 20th century progressed, advancing life expectancy rates meant retiring for five to ten years became more common. Clichés abound of grey nomads using this time to caravan around Australia, spend some time with the grandkids, maybe take up golf or lawn bowls, and perhaps go on a cruise or two.

Life expectancy (years) at birth by sex, 1881-1890 to 2013-2015

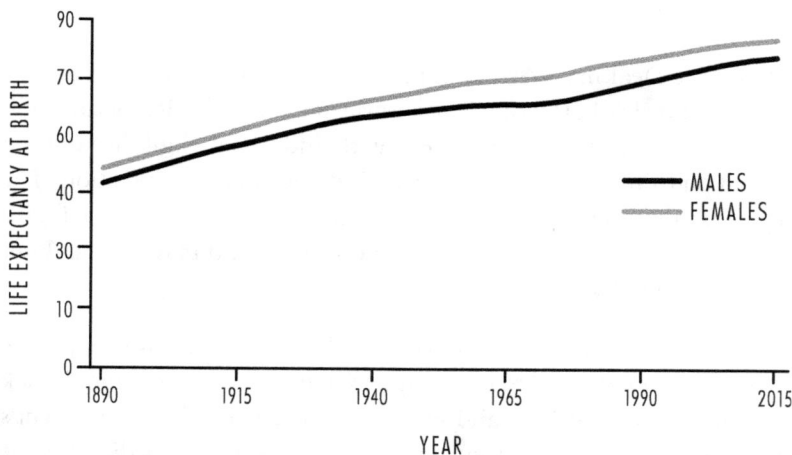

Source: Australian Bureau of Statistics, Australian Institute of Health and Welfare.

END OF THE RETIREMENT AGE

Fast-forward to today and average life expectancy at birth is 84.5 years for women and 80.4 years for men. Life expectancies have risen at a phenomenal rate since the Age Pension was introduced, and this has led to the bittersweet reality of more time on Earth, accompanied by the challenge of funding all those extra years. What should be an unequivocally positive development has become a source of angst, uncertainty and despair for individuals (and governments) who are financially ill-prepared for longer life spans. Pressure on the government continues to mount, and the cost to the federal budget is now estimated at $44 billion per year and rising. In other words, the welfare system has been left behind – straining under the weight of rising Age Pension commitments and the healthcare costs of a society growing older.

Australian economics writer Jessica Irvine laments this heightened dependence on social security, which is now the most significant expenditure item in the federal budget. In a November 2013 *Daily Telegraph* article titled 'With an ageing population should you reconsider your retirement plans?', Irvine wrote, 'The Age Pension, designed as a social safety net, has instead become a warm blanket that we cling to for an increasing proportion of our lives.'

Distortions created by longer life expectancies even prompted former Prime Minister Paul Keating to propose a 'longevity levy' on the basis that the superannuation system was not keeping up with the reality of an ageing population. In a May 2014 interview with Tony Jones on the ABC *Lateline* program, Keating said, 'You can't save under super for 30 years or 35 years and then live another 30 years from it. In other words, the pool can never be big enough to sustain you till your 90s.'

Much needs to change. First and foremost, we need a new retirement paradigm that will better serve us all.

REINVENTING
THE RETIREMENT PARADIGM

*'The mystery of human existence
lies not in just staying alive, but in finding
something to live for.'*

FYODOR DOSTOYEVSKY

In January 2017, the CEO of the Australian Super Funds Association, Dr Martin Fahy, delivered a keynote address at the Pritchitt Partners Annual Reception in Sydney discussing the outlook for the superannuation industry. Entitled 'Super 2017: What would good look like?', his presentation explored the opportunities and challenges ahead for super, and the indicators of a healthy retirement savings system.

Yet the most profound opinion Fahy offered that night had nothing to do with finance. Towards the end of the speech, he called on Australians to rethink their traditional beliefs about retirement in order to arrive at a definition that might better serve us all.

'We need someone to come forward with a higher purpose for retirement,' Fahy says. 'At the moment, we think about retirement as recreation, which means retirement is about consumption. It is essentially inwardly focused. In that setting, it is unfulfilling, it is very expensive, and it is economically draining. Somewhere out there, and I think this is a challenge for baby boomers... we need some way of transforming our concept of retirement away from recreation and associations with consumption, and towards a re-creation of a higher purpose that gives definition to retirement. That will sit uncomfortably with many people.'

Fahy is not talking about incremental changes to the definition of retirement. Instead, he is hinting at a transformational shift in community attitudes and societal structures, which would completely reframe this life stage. Rather than perceiving retirement as an ending characterised by decline, it should be reinvented as a wonderful opportunity; as a new beginning, full of promise.

Fahy nominated the baby boomers as the ones to lead this reinvention. 'We need them to re-conceptualise retirement away from a short five-year period of recreation into a 25 to 35-year engagement with a higher purpose,' he says.

Demographer Bernard Salt agrees. In an article for *The Australian* titled 'Ageing Australia: Pluses and minuses for a nation showing its age', Salt wrote, 'the problem is that old age has had bad PR for decades; after all, old age ultimately leads to death. Yet the perception need not be like this. Retirement and ageing can be seen as the best time in life, especially if services are fairly funded and if community attitudes encourage tolerance rather than judgement. I am hoping the baby boomers can weave their magic and re-engineer the way we think about ageing.'

This reinvention is not about slaving away at work, unfulfilled, until you can no longer continue. But it does question the practicality and desirability of spending 30-plus years with an exclusive focus on leisure.

The challenge now is rethinking how you spend this precious extra time, made possible by rising living standards, medical advances, technological breakthroughs and improvements in public education.

It is about treating this period as a beginning rather than an ending, and (health permitting) as an opportunity to pursue and achieve all of those things you have yet to achieve due to lack of time, lack of money or fear.

But it won't be easy.

Reinvention requires planning, research, reflection and motivation to begin to move towards a new reality. In order to visualise and create that new reality, you need to have a thorough understanding of the current situation and the challenges you face. You also need to gain insights into the forces that have led to this point. This will enable you to move with purpose in a new direction.

REVISITING OUR PATRIOTIC DUTY

*'Why would I retire? Sit at home and watch TV? No
thanks. I'd rather be out playing.'*

PAUL MCCARTNEY

It is 4:30pm on 11 May 2004, and former Federal Treasurer Peter
Costello is holding court during a press conference at Canberra's
Parliament House. As he discusses the details of the Coalition's latest federal budget, he makes reference to a new baby bonus payment
and extra funding for childcare places. One reporter asks, 'Is this a
breeding budget, Mr Costello? Are you the family-friendly Treasurer
saying "get out there and procreate"?'

Costello replied, 'Well, you know, if you can have children, it is a
good thing to do ... You should have, if you can, one for your husband, and one for your wife, and one for the country.'

The reporter asks whether that means those who only have two children are unpatriotic. In a line that would be picked up by news outlets around the world, Costello fired back with an unconventional
appeal to halt Australia's declining birth rate.

He said, 'You go home and do your patriotic duty tonight.'

Following Costello's creative invitation to families to have more
children, the total fertility rate did indeed rise, but the bounce was
short-lived. The total fertility rate measures the average number of

babies born to a woman during her reproductive lifetime, and you of course need a rate of at least 2.0 to achieve 'replacement' of both parents. In 2004, the total fertility rate was 1.8 and this rose to 2.0 in 2008 (a 30-year high), before falling again to 1.8 by 2016. This compares to the nation's total fertility rate in 1961 of 3.61. In other words, families are having around half as many children today as they were in the 1960s.

Total fertility rate, Australia, 1921-2006

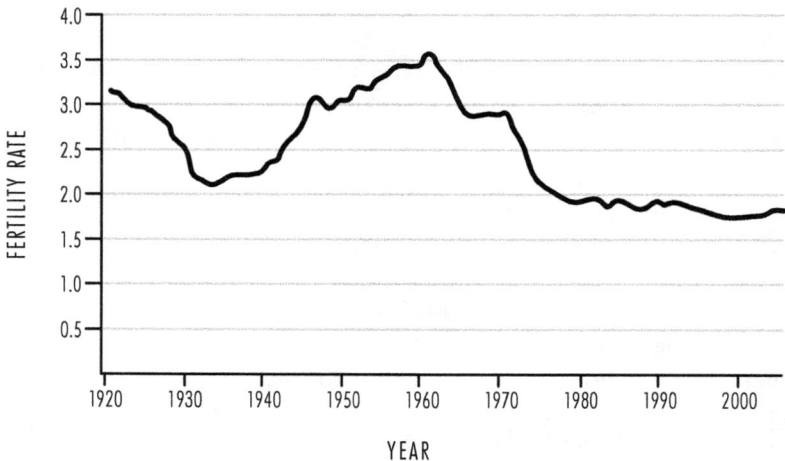

Source: Australian Bureau of Statistics, Australian Institute of Family Studies.

It is widely accepted that due to the changing composition of Australia's population, with each year that passes, the federal government is under increasing financial pressure, and is less able to meet rising demand for social security benefits. This economic inevitability arises due to the reality of fewer working-age taxpayers supporting a growing grey army of Age Pension recipients – a generation living longer than at any other time in history. Due to the combination of a post-war baby boom in the 1950s, and the more recent decline in fertility rates, we have unwittingly created a mathematical conundrum. While there used to be five working-age taxpayers for every retiree, before long there will be just two. Of this curly equation, Costello recently made the following glib statement on Channel Nine's *60 Minutes* program: 'We just can't carry that.'

But there is hope. Consider a modern-day equivalent of Costello's appeal for families to have one child for mum, one for dad, and one for the country. Rather than encouraging younger Australians to procreate in greater numbers, appealing to older Australians to reconsider their path to retirement might be a better solution to addressing the imbalance between taxpayers and Age Pension recipients.

That is, encouraging older Australians who are still working, and who are willing and able, to remain in the workforce for an additional three years of full-time, part-time or casual employment, relative to when they had planned to retire.

One year for yourself (for the social, financial and psychological benefits of remaining engaged in the workforce); one year for the long-term financial security of your family; and one year for your country, which prospers through additional tax receipts, an increase in national savings and a reduction in social security spending.

When Social Services Minister Christian Porter argues for increasing the Age Pension eligibility age from 67 to 70, he is effectively advocating the same thing. Suggestions that people work until age 70 are often met with howls of criticism; there is outrage at the prospect of people in manually intensive jobs being forced to continue back-breaking work until they drop dead. But we need a less emotive and more nuanced conversation about transitions and retraining as we move through our careers. The real problem is that the age of eligibility for the Age Pension has barely moved in 100 years, even though life expectancy has extended by decades in that time. Something has to give.

And in many ways, change is already underway, albeit slowly. Workforce participation rates among mature-age employees are steadily rising. Meanwhile, the idea of transitioning to eventual retirement via part-time work has become more popular since 2005, when new rules were introduced allowing over-55s to access their super while still at work.

Retirement rate, people aged 45 and over, by age, November 1997 to 2012-13

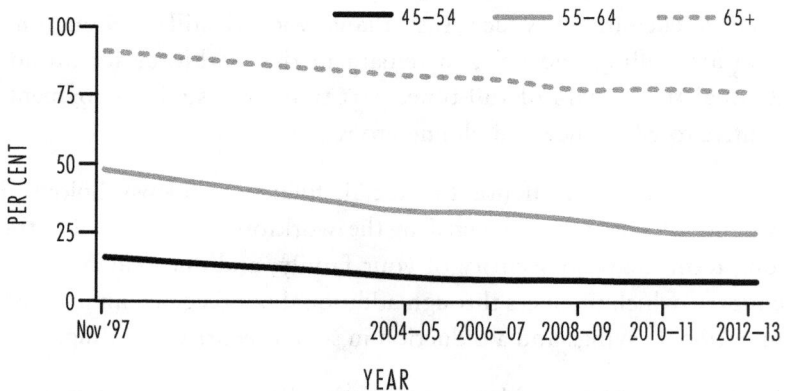

Source: Australian Bureau of Statistics, Australian Institute of Health and Welfare.

The above graph indicates Australians are slowly but surely choosing to retire later in life. In October 2016, Roy Morgan released research indicating that, over the past couple of years, the average age people were planning to retire had increased from 58 to 61. Directionally, these trends are positive, but as a nation we simply cannot afford for as many individuals to cease contributing to the tax base as early as age 61 – the money is just not there.

This is not to suggest that people work until they keel over. The idea that people 'work until they drop' is jarring because it takes away hope. We have an innate need to work towards milestones in life, and extreme prescriptions to work indefinitely are more likely to cause fear and despondency than serve as motivation to improve our position.

But by acknowledging the many additional years of average life expectancy we were afforded over the past 100 years, we have a choice as to whether we spend the entire time at leisure, or whether there is room for a more balanced combination of work and play in our 60s and 70s and beyond.

For every additional year that older Australians stay in the workforce, that's one extra year of contributing to the tax base (while boosting savings for eventual retirement), and one less year of drawing down on social security benefits. These are win-win outcomes; when we lift the mature-age participation rate in meaningful ways, the economic benefits are extraordinary.

A 2012 research report by Deloitte Access Economics, titled 'Increasing participation among older workers: the grey army advances', found that if Australia could achieve an additional three per cent lift in workforce participation among over-55s (relative to current expectations), the economic benefit to the nation would be some $33 billion, or 1.6 per cent of GDP by 2024-25. Meanwhile, a five per cent increase above and beyond current expectations over the same time frame would add $48 billion to GDP.

The report says, 'The latter would represent a major change in Australia's workforce, with participation among Australians in their 70s lifting by a half and participation among those aged 50-59 closing in on that of Australians in their 20s and 30s. It is therefore no surprise that the resulting economic benefits would rank with the gains that Australia has achieved from some of the major economic reforms of times past.'

And so we stand at an economic crossroads. If our glass is half-empty, economic stagnation lies ahead – driven by persistently low birth rates and an increasingly unproductive ageing population. But if our glass is half-full (and we're collectively up for the challenge), the possibility emerges of a renewal in participation and productivity among the healthiest-ever crop of Australians in their 50s, 60s and 70s. It just may be that we can look forward to a surprising new wave of economic prosperity – led by older Australians who are willing and able to contribute later in life, provided the opportunities exist to do so.

FOUR CONVERGING REALITIES CHALLENGING RETIREES

'There is nothing permanent except change.'

HERACLITUS

Our need to plan effectively for retirement didn't change dramatically for much of the 20th century, but the urgency is rising today. We are creatures who thrive on certainty, yet we've never lived in more ambiguous times.

As an existing or soon-to-be retiree, there are four challenges you face:

1. Longer life expectancies.
2. The decline of social security, resulting in increasingly drastic welfare cuts.
3. Dwindling job security and persistent workplace discrimination.
4. Planning for your financial future in a world obsessed with 'now'.

In others words, we're living for many more years and therefore having to fund a longer retirement, yet the main income sources we rely on in the workforce and beyond have never been more uncertain.

These converging realities mean two things. First, retirement – as experienced by previous generations – is increasingly unrecognisable.

Second, there has never been a more challenging time to undertake the financial and non-financial preparation that is essential if you are to thrive and maximise your wellbeing as you grow older.

Countless studies indicate that individuals who remain engaged and active in the community and the workplace as they age report higher levels of happiness, fulfilment and satisfaction in life. Unfortunately, technological change, workforce casualisation and age discrimination mean job security is rapidly becoming a thing of the past.

In an appearance on the Q&A program in October 2016, industrial relations expert and columnist Grace Collier said, 'There's really no such thing as secure, guaranteed employment for life. We are all at risk of being put out of work if we're not doing what we should be doing, or if our employer isn't profitable, or if our employer wants to [hire workers] offshore. This is the reality of modern life ... There's nobody in this room that has a guarantee of their job and of their income ... There's a bit of an adjustment happening in Australia. And in any correction, there is pain.'

The challenges for older Australians seeking to remain in the workforce are well documented. (We'll discuss some of those challenges in a later chapter.)

Then, after ceasing work, retirees are finding the government is incrementally – yet aggressively – winding back social security, as the nation simply cannot afford to continue on its current path. In January 2017, some 320,000 older Australians witnessed firsthand the tightening of the nation's fiscal belt, as individuals lost up to $9,000 in annual Age Pension payments, while couples lost up to $15,000 per year. The state of the nation's finances has deteriorated to a point where, collectively, we pay more than $12 billion per year in interest alone on the debt we owe, while spending on the Age Pension is forecast to balloon at an alarming rate. Our expectations for the level of government support in retirement must therefore be tempered, particularly if you have the means to support yourself.

Projection of Australian government spending on age-related pensions

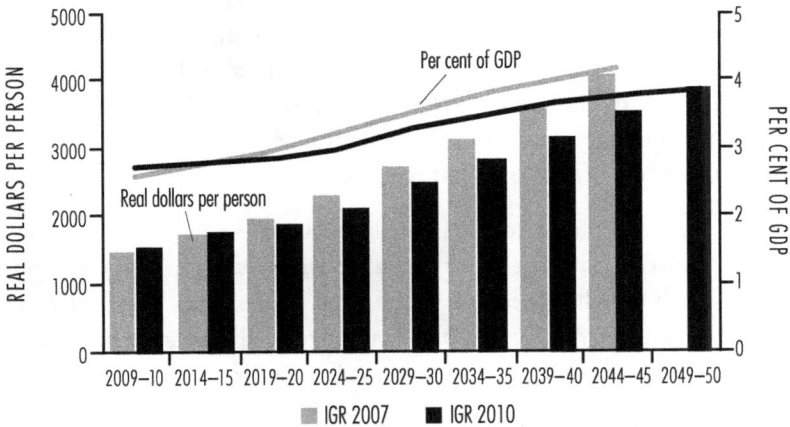

Source: Treasury projections.

Not only are your income sources less certain, but the backdrop to your life is increasingly noisy. Technologically driven, and based on an obsession with the 24-hour news cycle, nowhere is the chaos more prevalent than in financial markets. You are encouraged to plan with a 30-year retirement in mind, and to invest for the long term, yet news outlets breathlessly report the apparent significance of *hourly* movements on currencies and stock market indices. Short-termism is rife, which means financial decision-making is a minefield.

In a briefing paper titled 'The long and the short of it', Graham Rich, Dean of the PortfolioConstruction Forum, captures this madness with striking clarity.

He says, 'The world seems to operate on ever-shorter cycles. Politicians promise lower taxes (or union deals) to boost their election prospects, instead of proposing the infrastructure projects which could provide multi-decade economic and social benefits. Companies pay higher dividends and buy back their shares, rather than reinvesting profits for future growth. Public outrage flares and dissipates within hours, driven by the constant churn of social media. Meanwhile commentators bemoan the inability of governments, corporations and the general public to focus on what truly matters.'

When trying to plan effectively for how you are going to spend your life in retirement, there is a natural tension between a society obsessed with the short term, and the need to methodically and carefully prepare for the future. Looking beyond the noise is hard, and does not always come naturally, but it is essential as you grow older.

As human beings, we yearn for more certainty to maintain some semblance of control over the direction of our lives. In April 2017, entrepreneur and philanthropist Harold Mitchell wrote in *The Sydney Morning Herald* of the need for the federal government to stop fiddling with the superannuation system, to give people more certainty about the rules of the game as they save for retirement. In his article 'Equity is good, but cash is king in retirement', Mitchell says, 'There is plenty to be concerned about in the world without having to worry about how we can survive in old age. I have the feeling that we are living in an accelerating cycle of insecurity. It's one of the reasons governments and leaders come and go quicker than ever before.'

It was not that long ago that one-term governments at state and federal level were anomalies, as the electorate would, more often than not, give the sitting government sufficient time to implement its agenda. The opposite has occurred in recent years, as increasingly impatient voters send a message to politicians that they had better get it right the first time; there will be no second chances. The rise of what were once fringe parties, and the dilution of the primary vote for Labor and the Coalition, are confirmation of the electorate's unease.

The accelerating cycle of insecurity that Mitchell highlights is real – events involving politics, markets and technology seem to move ever faster. And when the world around us feels like it is constantly speeding up, we are left with an unnerving backdrop for planning ahead and making life's big decisions.

In his 2004 book, *In Praise of Slow*, author Carl Honoré laments society's growing focus on speed at the expense of better personal and community outcomes.

'In this media-drenched, data-rich, channel-surfing, computer-gaming age, we have lost the art of doing nothing, of shutting out the background noise and distractions, of slowing down and simply being alone with our thoughts. Boredom – the word itself hardly existed 150 years ago – is a modern invention. Remove all stimulation and we fidget, panic, and look for something, anything, to do to make use of the time. When did you last see someone just gazing out the window on a train? Everyone is too busy reading the paper, playing video games, working on the laptop, yammering into their mobile phones,' he says. 'Our impatience is so implacable that, as actress-author Carrie Fisher quipped, even "instant gratification takes too long."'

Speaking about his book in a 2005 TEDx Talk, Honoré observed, 'The supreme irony of publishing a book about slowness is that you have to go around promoting it really fast ... Because everyone these days wants to know how to slow down, but they want to know how to slow down really quickly ... Because that's kind of the world that we live in now, a world stuck in fast-forward.'

To add to your challenges, the hurdles to achieving financial success grow ever higher. It is no longer satisfactory to simply pay off the mortgage to achieve the Great Australian Dream – an unencumbered home is now just a ticket to the game. You also need to save enough over your working life to ensure a comfortable retirement. The need to generate a sustainable, life-enriching retirement income is the biggest financial-planning challenge of your time.

These realities conspire to make today the most challenging time in history to prepare effectively for life beyond traditional employment.

But there is hope...

FINDING MEANING AND PURPOSE

'People who look forward to retirement aren't enjoying their life as much as I am.'

MORGAN FREEMAN

The way in which you understand and frame these challenges, and the mindset you choose to adopt in overcoming them, will contribute greatly to the outcomes you achieve and the wellbeing you experience in retirement. If you understand the retirement playing field and equip yourself with the right knowledge, you can make your retirement transition a transformational phase of your life, rather than an exercise in survival.

You have two choices. You can frame these forces as negatives, or you can make a conscious choice to become better informed about the environment in which you will one day transition (whatever that looks like for you), and adapt your plan accordingly. In order to do this, you must first understand what is driving each force. Once you gain deeper insights into these issues, you begin to see the opportunities. I speak to hundreds of people in their 50s, 60s, 70s and beyond every year about their plans and priorities for the future. The recurring theme is that the earlier you start thinking about how you would like your life to look as you grow older, the more choice and flexibility you will enjoy as you age, and the more likely you are to thrive and achieve the things in life that matter to you.

You have the opportunity to visualise the next phase of your life in new ways that will better serve you. Retirement is too often associated with endings. You need to redefine it as the beginning, and as an opportunity to live your life on purpose. Everyone craves meaning, purpose and fulfilment in their 'encore years', but there is no handbook to obtain those things ... until now.

One of the aims of this book is to help you understand the challenges and opportunities of the new retirement playing field, and to provide insights, stories and strategies to help you adapt and thrive in this new reality. A key message I want to highlight is that preparing for the retirement years is about so much more than financial planning. Done well, it involves consciously planning all aspects of your life so that you live meaningfully and purposefully for what is, on average, a multi-decade period.

Rather than provide a new framework for retirement, I want to share stories about the way retirement is *already* being redefined by Australians from all walks of life in their 50s, 60s and 70s. Despite the four major challenges confronting you, humans have a tendency to adapt to changing environments, which means a new and more meaningful definition of retirement is emerging – one that is more colourful, varied and useful than the original.

In the chapters that follow, you'll gain a deeper understanding of the four realities shaping the modern retirement landscape. Then, through the stories and experiences of others, my aim is to help you answer the following questions:

- What are some of the ways you might reframe retirement so it better serves you?

- How is retirement evolving, and in what ways are Australians in their 50s, 60s and 70s already redefining retirement on their terms?
- Most importantly, how can you ensure meaning, purpose and wellbeing in your encore years?

The retirement age is over. What takes its place has the potential to be transformational.

Let's get to work.

PART 1

CONTENDING WITH LONGER LIFE EXPECTANCIES

VISUALISING THE FUTURE

'Once you're over the hill, you begin to pick up speed.'

CHARLES M. SCHULZ

Gains in average life expectancy over the last 100 years have been nothing short of remarkable. Improvements achieved in the first half of the 20th century were driven mainly by reduced infant mortality, declines in deaths from infections, and better sanitation. More recent gains in average life expectancy are attributed to continued rising prosperity, improved healthcare, reduced smoking rates, and advances in medical technology, which allow for more timely and accurate diagnostics and more successful treatments.

The end result is that, in the space of 100 years, the average life expectancy has risen from 55 years to 80 years for men, and from 59 years to 84 years for women.

So, where to from here? Broadly speaking, there are two camps of research – the 'exponential' camp and the 'incremental' camp – each offering predictions on where life expectancy trends may ultimately go in the decades ahead.

The exponential camp is characterised by 'moon-shot' predictions driven by cutting-edge science and cashed-up biotechnology companies, marketing themselves as 'perilously close' to breakthroughs that will make living to 100 the new normal. Such activity often involves some combination of genomics, cell therapy, machine learning and genetic editing, and the anticipated gains in longevity are predicted to be exponential.

Sitting firmly in the exponential camp is Dr Peter Diamandis. In March 2014, Diamandis, along with John Craig Venter and Robert Hariri, raised $80 million to launch Human Longevity, Inc. (HLI) – a company focused on extending the healthy human life span. HLI aims to 'extend healthy human life by revolutionising human health and transforming the practice of human medicine.'

Diamandis seems impressed, but ultimately dissatisfied, with advances made in average life expectancy until now. 'Between 1910 and 2010, improvements in medicine and sanitation increased the human life span [in the United States] by 50 per cent from 50 to 75 years. Today, with the emergence of exponential technologies such as those being pioneered and advanced by HLI, we have the potential to meaningfully extend the life span even further,' he says.

In a December 2016 TEDx Talk in Los Angeles, titled 'Imagining the Future: The Transformation of Humanity', Diamandis highlighted the magnitude of the changes the science may enable.

'Through genomics and stem cell science ... our mission is to add 30-40 healthy years onto your life. To give you the aesthetics, the cognition and the mobility at 100 that you had at 60. And if you get that, we're heading towards a world of an indefinite life span. These are crazy ideas. But they're coming because the tools we have to enable them are accelerating faster than we could possibly know.'

Yet, during interviews conducted for this book, it became clear that many people are uncomfortable about the prospect of substantially longer life spans, because it challenges everything we have ever assumed about the major milestones in life and a 'normal' passage through the life cycle. Life is uncertain enough, and imagining a world where we routinely live to 120 creates many additional layers of ambiguity that are difficult to fathom, let alone get excited about. A dramatically longer life expectancy also holds little appeal if it is accompanied by poor health and declining levels of wellbeing.

While Diamandis describes as 'crazy' the idea that, one day, 100 may be the new 60, investors are taking the scientific potential of HLI's activities very seriously. In April 2016, the company successfully raised a further $220 million from a host of prominent venture capital firms and individual investors (valuing the company at $1.2 billion), all willing to back the technology that has the potential to make our current passage through the life cycle a thing of the past.

While the incremental camp also predicts continued increases in life expectancy, it is at a far steadier and more predictable pace. For example, research published in *The Lancet* medical journal, titled 'Future life expectancy in 35 industrialised countries: projections with a Bayesian model ensemble', concluded, 'There is more than a 50 per cent probability that by 2030, national female life expectancy will break the 90-year barrier, a level that was deemed unattainable by some at the turn of the 21st century.'

Of the 35 industrialised countries included in the study, South Korea is the standout. The average life expectancy of South Korean women has increased by around 3.7 years every decade since the mid-1980s, when they were ranked 29th, and the likelihood is that South Korean women will have the world's longest life expectancy at birth by the year 2030. For men, the top three countries with the longest projected life expectancy at birth in 2030 are South Korea, Australia and Switzerland.

We can learn much from the South Korean ascension to the top of the longevity charts. Such strong gains are attributed to factors such as better access to healthcare, and the postponement of death from chronic diseases thanks to improved diagnostic technology and treatment methods. Rising prosperity and education standards are credited with driving improvements in nutrition. It is also worth noting that the South Korean population has a lower body mass index, lower blood pressure statistics, and fewer female smokers than other industrialised countries included in the study.

These findings point to another topic that often comes up in the conversation about longevity trends: the fact that women are currently expected to comfortably outlive men. In Australia, data from the Australian Bureau of Statistics indicates that life expectancy is at record highs, with newborn females expected to live until 84.5, while males are expected to live until 80.4 – a gap of 4.1 years.

Intriguingly, this gap in life expectancy between men and women is closing in most countries. Australia is a case in point. In 2010, the female-male difference was around 4.5 years, yet by 2030 the difference is predicted to reduce to just 3.5 years.

The above article points out: 'The current gender differences in life expectancy are due to differences in deaths from external causes (injuries) and from conditions such as lung cancer and cardiovascular diseases, whose risk factors (e.g. smoking) have different trends in men and women.'

THE BUSINESS OF EXPANDING
THE HUMAN LIFE SPAN

*'Change is the law of life. And those who look only to
the past or present are certain to miss the future.'*

JOHN F. KENNEDY

Hamish Douglass, Chief Executive Officer and Lead Portfolio Manager at Magellan Financial Group, has also weighed in on life expectancy trends, albeit from a slightly different perspective.

Magellan invests in some of the world's leading technology companies (at the time of writing, Apple Inc is the Magellan Global Fund's largest holding). Increasingly, the company's investment strategy is influenced by where Douglass sees technological trends going – in an attempt to identify companies that may be the potential winners and losers of the future. Provided shares in those companies can be purchased at a reasonable valuation, Magellan invests accordingly.

Now more than ever, Douglass believes that such is the pace of technological change, it is critical to understand the future in order to adapt your investment priorities and make better informed financial decisions, based on how society may evolve. In the 2016 Magellan Global Annual Investor Report, he refers to Google co-founder Larry Page, who attributes the failure of once-iconic companies like Kodak and Nokia to the idea that they simply 'missed the future'.

In September 2016, at an investment forum in Sydney, Douglass discussed his thoughts on historical life expectancy trends, and, more intriguingly, the potential impact of science and modern medicine on life expectancy in the future.

'I would say particularly now we have fully sequenced the human genome and it has become incredibly cost-effective, and we now can combine this with artificial intelligence and image recognition and mass data assimilation, with very specialised medicine[s], it would appear that we are probably going to make quicker advances in medical science than has been possible in the past,' he said.

'And what that probably means is if you're curing illnesses, people on average will live longer and maybe we're going to have life expectancy – within 20 years – of over 100, and I think that's fairly realistic. It's not going to happen as fast as the digital assistant is going to happen, because even if you make a breakthrough there is a long regulatory approval to get new science approved, so this is going to happen at a slower pace than other forms of technology. But is that where it ends?'

Douglass spoke of a future that is perhaps 20 to 30 years away, where the combination of printable organs and epigenetics allows science and technology to intervene in the ageing process to extend average life expectancy well beyond 100.

'There is an enormous amount of money going into radical life-extension thinking. Google has a business that is dedicated to radical life extensions. They're really trying to understand what causes ageing. There's a lot of science going to epigenetics, gene editing and nanotechnology. Epigenetics is the science of gene expression. Certain genes in our body do very, very important things. It appears, according to a number of scientists who are specialists in this area [that], as we age, certain genes are either turned on or off that cause the ageing process. So, we may be genetically programmed to effectively die biologically by turning on genes that cause inflammation and ageing.

'The science of epigenetics is actually, through gene sequencing, trying to understand exactly which genes do what and then influencing those genes to never turn themselves on or off, particularly the ones that cause ageing.'

Douglass's keen interest in future life expectancy trends suggests that eventually, the impact of significantly longer life spans will reverberate across the corporate world. A drastically altered passage through the life cycle has the potential to redefine the bounds of competition in countless industries – creating new winners and losers on financial markets.

EXPLORING A CURE FOR AGEING

'It's paradoxical that the idea of living a long life appeals to everyone, but the idea of getting old doesn't appeal to anyone.'

ANDY ROONEY

Professor David Sinclair, who holds a PhD in molecular genetics and is co-founder and co-chief of the scientific journal *Aging*, is also fiercely passionate about slowing down the ageing process to allow people to live longer, healthier lives.

Sinclair undertakes dual roles as a Professor at the School of Medicine at the University of New South Wales, and as a Professor in the Genetic Department at Harvard Medical School in Boston. He has also founded and sold a number of pharmaceutical and biotechnology companies.

Among many breakthroughs, he is renowned for his research into the link between an anti-ageing enzyme known as 'SIRT1' and a molecule found in red wine called resveratrol, though he cautions against overindulging, suggesting you would need to drink 100 glasses of red wine a day to derive any therapeutic benefit!

Sinclair has discovered longevity genes that can actually protect your body from ageing. He indicates these genes can be modified so they become more active and potentially delay the diseases you typically succumb to as you get older, thereby arresting the ageing process.

He believes you are only given 'one precious life, and it is a life to be embraced, a life to be used for good, and a life that is worth prolonging, in good health.'

It is May 2013, and Sinclair is on stage at the Sydney Opera House to deliver a TEDx Talk titled 'A Cure for Ageing?' As he stands before a crowd of 2,200 attendees and a vast global online audience, he recalls a memory of his daughter, Madeline, when she was just four years old. He describes putting his daughter to bed one night when she asks him, 'Daddy, will you always be around to protect me?' Emotional, Sinclair describes his response: 'I'm sorry. One day, like everybody, I will grow old, and I will die.' He watched as Madeline's eyes welled up. She proceeded to give him an almighty hug, and, as many parents do, he went on to comfort his inquisitive daughter by urging her not to fill her head with such existential questions.

But as a scientist, Sinclair despairs at a society that shies away from speaking frankly about ageing and death. 'We all try to forget about this truth and ironically I believe this is actually preventing us from realising the lives we could actually live,' he says.

Sinclair advocates strongly for research into the genetic causes of ageing, rather than devoting so many resources to seeking cures for individual diseases. He claims we should be up in arms about the universal 'disease' of ageing, and he feels he has an economic and moral duty to use his scientific expertise to work towards a solution.

'A fraction of medical research, just one per cent, is devoted to why we age. Alzheimer's, cancer, heart disease – these are natural, and we do everything we can to prevent and slow these diseases down. Ninety-nine per cent of medical research is devoted to trying to slow down these diseases, which only a fraction of us actually get. Whereas ageing, if we're lucky, affects all of us,' he says.

'What we've ended up with is a nation of elderly [people], whose hearts are working well, for example, but their brains are no longer functioning, and this is a major problem for our healthcare system. It's extremely, extremely expensive. What we need are medicines that will keep all our body parts working at the same time. If we just fix one part of the body, the problem is that some other part will break down. We're just switching our diseases. And I don't think this is the right way to go about it.'

While the advances in average life expectancy over the last 100 years are nothing short of extraordinary, if Sinclair achieves his aims, it may signal that the best is yet to come. In a July 2016 interview with *Ageing Reversed*, he looks forward to a future where 90-year-olds still play tennis and are every bit as healthy as 50-year-olds. If the scientific breakthroughs continue, he expects many more people will live to 100 while enjoying a far superior quality of life to today's centenarians; perhaps even watching their great-grandchildren graduate from university.

'I'm optimistic the science is solid and the field of ageing is now at the forefront of biology, and if I'm not successful and these drugs don't end up on the market, I think someone will have a breakthrough. We've had the paradigm shift. We know it's possible. It's just a matter of time that we will have these remarkable drugs to treat the elderly and the sick. I have to be frank – I don't know if this is going to be successful but I do know that it will be possible one day. Maybe in the next few years or maybe it's another few decades. I don't know but we've certainly turned a corner and I think that the future of humanity looks bright if we can have medicines like this. I think dying in your 60s or being frail in your 80s may be a thing of the past and I hope to see that in my lifetime,' says Sinclair.

But not everyone is enamoured by the prospect of dramatic leaps in average life expectancy. Negative reactions to the idea are common, due to the assumption that any additional years are unlikely to offer a sufficient quality of life to be enjoyable. After all, it is not considered compelling to simply increase average life spans in the absence of any meaningful advances in health and wellbeing.

In October 2015, John Zubrzycki wrote an article for *The Sydney Morning Herald* titled 'Never say die: David Sinclair's anti-ageing quest'. Zubrzycki points to a significant degree of cynicism about the idea of longer life spans, and a reluctance to embrace such advancements.

'The public ... is sceptical,' he says. 'A 2011 survey found that while 65 per cent of Australians supported research that would slow ageing, only 35 per cent said they would use life-extension technology if one became available. Nearly half of those polled believed that developing life-extension technologies would do more harm than good to society overall.'

Fast-forward to March 2017, and Sinclair and his team make worldwide headlines with a scientific breakthrough that could be the beginning of a revolutionary drug that has the potential to reverse the ageing process.

Through a series of experiments with mice, the team demonstrate that it is possible to arrest the decline of your cells over time and achieve DNA repair, which has the potential to reverse damage done by exposure to radiation or ageing. The results are sufficiently compelling that human trials are scheduled to get underway.

'The cells of the old mice were indistinguishable from the young mice, after just one week of treatment,' Sinclair says. 'This is the closest we are to a safe and effective anti-ageing drug that's perhaps only three to five years away from being on the market if the trials go well.'

While anti-ageing pills may have been regarded as the stuff of science fiction until now, when you combine the exponential rate of technological change with the determination and ingenuity of scientists like David Sinclair, we may need to completely rethink the bounds of possibility in our lifetime.

JOINING THE DOTS
ON WHERE THE SCIENCE MAY GO

*'The afternoon of human life must also have
a significance of its own and cannot be merely
a pitiful appendage to life's morning.'*

CARL JUNG

Viewed in isolation, many technological advancements tend to lead to incremental improvements, but exponential gains are possible when pioneering technologies come together in the right way at the right time. Mobile phones, internet browsers, MP3 players, touchscreen technology and digital cameras existed in isolation long before Steve Jobs put them together in the form of the iPhone in June 2007.

Upon the iPhone's release, former Microsoft chief executive Steve Ballmer famously predicted, 'There's no chance the iPhone is going to get any significant market share. No chance.' As history shows, the iPhone would go on to change the world, with more than 1.2 billion units sold between 2007 and 2017, as Apple became the world's most profitable company.

In the same way, a scientific convergence is underway that could one day lead to transformational advances in longevity. While David Sinclair pursues genetic modification and DNA repair as a means to slowing the ageing process, scientists at the University of California are busily working out how to print three-dimensional organs that may one day serve as fully functioning 'spare parts' for the human body.

You only need to look at national waiting lists for organ transplants to appreciate the life-saving potential of technology that can create effective artificial organs. According to the Australian Regenerative Medicine Institute, there are around 1,600 Australians on the organ transplant waiting list at any time. But as there are too few donor organs available, sadly, many on the waiting list die before receiving a life-saving transplant.

In 1954, Nobel laureate Dr Joseph E. Murray and his colleagues completed the first ever successful human organ transplant, by transplanting a kidney from one identical twin to another in Brigham Hospital in Boston. More than 50 years later, in an interview with the New York Organ Donor Network publication, *On the Beat,* Murray is asked for his views on the current state of organ donation. He says, 'I think it is just a fact of life that there aren't enough [organs] to go around. All we've got to do is make organs, and this is the stuff we are already doing at MIT and Harvard, trying to lay a framework for creating organs.'

The scientific race is now on to create fully functioning artificial organs that can be transferred into humans to replace worn-out body parts. In simple terms, the aim is to create replacement organs from an individual's own cells and tissues in order to address the lack of donor organs, while ideally reducing risks and complications that typically arise where a recipient's body rejects the donor organ.

Historically, there have been three main challenges when scientists have attempted to create organs. The first is no different from the challenges faced when transplanting a donor organ – the recipient's body must 'accept' the external organ so it operates in harmony with the rest of their inner workings. The second challenge is ensuring enough cells can be grown outside the recipient's body to form the basis of the artificial organ. The third problem arises as organs need a healthy flow of blood in order to survive, and the only way to achieve this is through the creation of intricate networks of blood vessels that are incredibly difficult to build, and even harder to integrate into the human body to enable a fully functioning organ with a sufficient flow of oxygen and nutrients. This is known as 'vascularity' and, until now, it has been the biggest hurdle for scientists to overcome in building successful 3D printed human organs.

In March 2017, Dr Shaochen Chen, a Professor in the Nanoengineering Department at the University of California, led a team that used 3D printing to successfully create a blood vessel network that could lead to breakthroughs in more widespread creation of artificial organs.

In an interview with *Science Daily*, he said, 'Almost all tissues and organs need blood vessels to survive and work properly. This is a big bottleneck in making organ transplants, which are in high demand but in short supply. 3D bioprinting organs can help bridge this gap, and our lab has taken a big step towards that goal.'

That such microscopic blood vessel structures can be designed on a computer program – and ultimately printed into existence in a matter of seconds – is mind-blowing. And while it is likely we are still some years from clinical trials and possible widespread availability of artificial organ replacement, you get the sense that with so much intellectual firepower focused on the problem, it is only a matter of time.

If you consider the combination of David Sinclair's pioneering work in genetic modification – which could literally slow the ageing process – and Shaochen Chen's efforts to create 3D printed organs, enabling replacement of worn-out body parts – you begin to see what may ultimately be possible in the quest to extend the healthy human life span.

CLUES TO BOOST YOUR CHANCES OF A LONGER LIFE

*'I could be 100 years old and in my rocker,
but I'll still be very proud that I was part of the
Harry Potter films.'*

EMMA WATSON

Living to be 100 years old has always been considered a remarkable achievement, and, according to the government's 2015 Intergenerational Report, it is likely to become more commonplace.

In 1975, the number of Australians aged over 85 was around 80,000, or less than one per cent of the population. By 2055, the Intergenerational Report forecasts that close to two million Australians will be over 85 (around five per cent of the population), and 40,000 of those are projected to live to 100.

'This is a dramatic increase, well over 300 times the 122 Australian centenarians in 1974-75,' the report says.

For now, living to 100 remains rare. But as long as we remain a constitutional monarchy, the Queen may need to employ more staff to prepare congratulatory birthday messages to a growing band of Australian centenarians!

In November 2016, Italian woman Emma Morano celebrated her 117th birthday in her small apartment in the Italian town of Verbania.

Born in 1899, she was officially known as the world's oldest living person until her death in April 2017.

According to Guinness World Records, 'She joined our celebrated hall of fame with her amazing achievement when she was announced in 2016 as the oldest living female, and was officially confirmed as the last person to be born in the 1800s.'

Morano's life was a source of fascination and wonderment as she continued to defy records and achieve milestones rarely seen. In a 2015 interview with Elisabetta Povoledo of *The New York Times*, Morano, the eldest of eight children, reflects on simple pleasures while growing up. 'My sisters and I loved to dance and we'd run away to the dance hall and then our mother would come looking for us with a birch stick,' she said.

Yet it was her rather unusual diet that was of most interest to those curious about the daily habits of someone who managed to live such a long life. In a 2015 interview with Italian newspaper *La Stampa*, she provided details of her typical daily food intake. 'For breakfast I eat biscuits with milk or water. Then during the day, I eat two eggs – one raw and one cooked – just like the doctor recommended when I was 20 years old. For lunch, I'll eat pasta and minced meat, then for dinner I'll just have a glass of milk.' In the same interview, Emma confirmed she goes to bed by 7pm each night and usually rises by 6am each morning.

Over the years, Morano has often been asked about the key to her longevity, and she points to a range of reasons. She never used drugs, but she enjoyed the odd glass of homemade brandy and the occasional chocolate. Perhaps most significantly, she believed it was essential to always think positively about the future. Of course, that is easier said than done, especially for someone like Morano, who experienced her fair share of personal tragedy, and the hardship of two world wars and the Great Depression.

Povoledo writes, 'She is convinced that being single for most of her life, after an unhappy marriage that ended in 1938 following the death of an infant son, has kept her kicking ... She had plenty of suitors after that, but never chose another partner.'

Perhaps Emma Morano was ahead of her time when it came to choosing her retirement age. She worked in the kitchen of a boarding school in Verbania until deciding to retire at age 75.

Stories like Morano's capture the imagination because they challenge our understanding of the typical milestones we might expect and plan for as part of a 'normal' life span. Intuitively, we know such cases are statistical outliers, but we are nonetheless intrigued – even hopeful – about what we may be able to learn by studying centenarians in more detail. We wonder whether something in her routine or diet or lifestyle may be the secret to living such a long life.

While Morano's preference for raw eggs may not be the holy grail of increasing your longevity, over the years, a number of studies have identified pockets of the globe where living to 100 is unusually common. We should be careful in drawing conclusions from such cases, as above-average longevity is widely considered to be a function of a complex combination of genetics, diet, lifestyle and luck. But where clusters of individuals are identified as living beyond the average life expectancy over an extended period of time, chances are we are not dealing with a statistical anomaly, and there are indeed lessons we can learn, and recurring themes we can draw on, that may provide clues to some of the inputs to a longer life span.

One such location is Okinawa, a series of islands between Taiwan and Japan, where residents are renowned for living longer, healthier lives than the rest of the Japanese population and the Western world. The Okinawa Centenarian Study began in 1975, and has since examined the lives of more than 900 Okinawans who lived to 100 and beyond.

While residents of Okinawa have historically lived longer than average lives, most importantly, they have also lived *healthier* lives as they have aged. This is significant because, in any conversation I have had in researching this book, people are only excited by the idea of a longer life span if those extra years can be spent enjoyably, in good health. There is little appeal of living into your 90s if your later years are plagued by ill-health and immobility.

Differences in health outcomes between Okinawans and the Western world, in particular, are stark. During the study, Okinawans were found to experience around 80 per cent fewer cases of heart disease, breast and prostate cancer, and around half the level of ovarian and colon cancers when compared to North Americans.

In March 2002, the authors of the study, Dr Craig Willcox, Dr Bradley Willcox and Dr Makoto Suzuki, published a book called *The Okinawa Program*, which contrasted the health outcomes experienced in the Western world with those of the Okinawan population. They concluded, 'If Americans lived more like the Okinawans, 80 per cent of the nation's coronary care units, one-third of the cancer wards, and a lot of the nursing homes would be shut down.'

The Centenarian Study found that the factors contributing to such results include a low-calorie, mostly plant-based diet of just 1,800 calories per day (Okinawans practice calorie control via a philosophy known as 'hara hachi bu', which means you only eat until you are 80 per cent full), a high fruit and vegetable intake, consuming lots of omega-3s and other good fats, and an emphasis on consuming a high level of fibre and antioxidants. Not surprisingly, when combined with a lifestyle of regular physical activity, such a disciplined approach to food sees Okinawans exhibit a lower than average body mass index, and a seemingly slower ageing process. Even common diseases of ageing, such as dementia, are less prevalent in Okinawa relative to elderly populations in other developed countries.

While genetics and diet play a major role in life expectancy outcomes, we can also learn much from the Okinawans' focus on their psychological health. In a September 2009 TEDx Talk in Minnesota, author Dan Buettner touches on the notion of 'purpose' as potentially contributing just as much to Okinawan longevity as more measurable factors such as diet and exercise.

He says, 'In the Okinawan language (dialect), there is not even a word for retirement. Instead there is one word that imbues your entire life, and that word is "Ikigai". And, roughly translated, it means "the reason for which you wake up in the morning" ... You know the two most dangerous years in your life are the year you're born, because of infant mortality, and the year you retire. These people know their sense of purpose, and that's worth about seven years of extra life expectancy.'

While there is no universal formula that guarantees a longer life span, here is a summary that captures the Okinawan way of life:

- Regular physical activity, which is more likely to be incidental to daily activities (walking, fishing, and so on) as opposed to formal exercise.

- A mostly plant-based diet that is low in salt, and high in antioxidants via fruit, vegetables, nuts, fish, seaweed, fibre and soy.

- Lower than average calorie intake and a conscious effort to avoid overeating.

- Strong focus on identifying your sense of purpose in life (at all ages) and using that to anchor your psychological wellbeing.

- Nurturing your network of family and friends.

- Valuing older members of society highly and holding them in great esteem.

- Emphasis on T'ai-Chi and mindfulness to assist your mental state.

- Volunteering as means of developing your spirituality.

The future direction of life expectancy trends is clear. The only unknown is the rate of change that will occur, and the impact this will have on each of us in the years ahead. Over the past 100 years, the milestones of life have been progressively redefined. In an age of ever-increasing life spans, at some point we all need to decide *how* we will spend that precious extra time on Earth. While it may be a decidedly one-dimensional existence if those extra years are spent exclusively focused on work, there are valid reasons why spending decades entirely at leisure may be just as unfulfilling.

This is a choice about the gift of time. In *Why Milestones Matter: Time, Social Meaning and the Measure of the Moral Life*, Scott Stephens (the ABC's Religion and Ethics Editor) and Lisa A. Williams (Senior Lecturer in social psychology at the University of New South Wales) discuss the contrasting ways we can think about time.

'The predominant way we think about time these days is as a scarce commodity that we dare not waste and therefore from which we must extract maximal achievements, experience or profit. We could call this a *capitalist* conception of time. But then there is the *teleological* or *purposive* notion that time is the gift given to us during which to pursue a "complete life" – a profoundly Aristotelian notion bound up with the cultivation of virtue and the achievement of happiness. We would probably call it a *life well-lived*.'

As you'll discover in later chapters, the current generation of retirees have been busily redefining the retirement life stage. One of the emerging themes is the appeal of a lifestyle that comprises a unique balance of work *and* play, which may extend well beyond the traditional retirement age. It is becoming more common to remain involved in some form of paid or unpaid employment, but in a way that allows lifestyle flexibility and, critically, time to participate in a range of other activities.

Of course, the balance you strike between work and play will be unique to your own set of circumstances, values and priorities. However, the earlier you start thinking about how you will derive meaning and purpose from the way you spend your time, the better equipped you will be to thrive as you grow older.

PART 2

SURVIVING WITHOUT WELFARE

THE COST OF LIVING LONGER

*'The cost of living is nothing compared
to the cost of living longer.'*

JEREMY COOPER

We have established that in all likelihood, average life spans will
continue to increase in the years ahead. The only unknown is whether change will occur in an orderly, predictable, incremental way, or
whether the likes of Professor David Sinclair and his peers will indeed achieve game-changing scientific breakthroughs, which might
mean living to 100 years of age becomes the new normal.

Stemming from that is the issue of social security, or welfare, which,
in many Western countries (including Australia), is becoming more
and more scarce as governments struggle to support their ageing
populations.

As stated in the introduction, the challenge of an ageing population
is the diminishing ratio of taxpayers to support a growing number of
ageing social security recipients. The greater the mismatch between
these two groups, the more difficult it becomes to drive economic
growth through advancements in productivity, and the more pressure
the federal government feels as it attempts to balance the budget.

So much needs to change, lest we jeopardise our very standard of
living – and that of future generations. Already younger Australians
wonder whether any Age Pension will exist by the time they retire. A
2017 HSBC study, titled 'The Future of Retirement: Shifting Sands',

found 58 per cent of the 18,000 people surveyed globally believe the Millennial generation (those born between 1980 and 1997) are paying for the economic mistakes of older generations, such as the global financial crisis and rising debt levels.

Meanwhile, some older Australians (yourself included, perhaps) have experienced hefty pay cuts in recent years as the government tightens the eligibility criteria for the Age Pension.

So while we are living longer, the sustainability of a key source of income for around 80 per cent of Australia's retirees is becoming increasingly uncertain.

In May 2016, Tony Shepherd, an Australian business leader and former head of the National Commission of Audit, wrote an article for *The Sydney Morning Herald* titled 'Are the Baby Boomers the greediest generation ever?' He neatly sums up the moving parts that lock in the fiscal challenges of our ageing population.

'We have an ageing population, increasing life expectancy, an aged pension benchmarked to average male weekly earnings (the highest possible index) and the family home excluded from the asset test. The Age Pension costs us $42 billion a year and is estimated to grow at six per cent a year over the next 10 years – far higher than any predictions of inflation, GDP growth and real wage growth,' he says.

You could not hope for a more profound summary of the challenges we face in maintaining our standard of living, and that of future generations, and Shepherd's comments serve as useful context for much of the government belt-tightening that is underway.

If you're unsure which belt-tightening measures I'm referring to, and how they might affect you, the following case study should provide some clarification.

THE AGE PENSION INCOME HIT

Mary is a 68-year-old retiree from Sydney's southern suburbs. She lives alone in a modest apartment with an additional $550,000 in investment and personal assets. Her assets include $330,000 in a superannuation pension, from which she draws $16,500 per year, and a small investment unit worth around $200,000, which provides income of $8,000 per year. For Centrelink purposes, her car and personal assets are valued at $20,000. Prior to January 2017, Mary also received approximately $9,000 per year as a part Age Pension payment, which meant her total income was around $33,500 per year.

But following changes announced by Joe Hockey in the 2015 federal budget – and passed in the Senate later that year with the support of the Greens – from January 2017, Mary no longer receives any Age Pension support. She has lost around $9,000 per year in Age Pension payments, as well as her entitlement to a Pensioner Concession Card, which means she also loses a range of valuable subsidies and discounts valued at hundreds, if not thousands, of dollars per year.

If she would like to maintain the level of household income to which she is accustomed, Mary's only option is to draw an additional $9,000 per year from her superannuation pension (equivalent to withdrawing an extra 2.73% per annum of her balance), in order to offset the reduction in Age Pension payments. In an environment of record low interest rates, she will still manage to meet her ongoing living expenses, but the proportion of her spending funded by her own financial resources will increase substantially, and she will go through much more of her own capital during the course of her retirement.

By implementing these reforms, Canberra is sending a very strong signal that the trajectory of the nation's finances is unsustainable, and that we can no longer afford for annual growth in Age Pension expenditure to continue at the same rate. That means if you are considered to have sufficient means, there's a growing expectation to support yourself rather than relying on taxpayer-funded social security benefits.

These are some of the most substantial changes to Age Pension eligibility in history. And while the government of the day is, at times, portrayed as cruel, these cuts are just one element of a broader program of reform, which is making it increasingly difficult to obtain social security of any sort.

An assessment of Mary's financial position can only ever be a subjective judgement, and opinions vary widely about how effectively targeted the recent Age Pension reforms were. For context, the Association of Superannuation Funds of Australia (ASFA) publishes a quarterly benchmark of retirement income adequacy, as shown in the table below:

Budgets for various households and living standards for those aged around 65 (March quarter 2017, ASFA Retirement Standard)

	MODEST LIFESTYLE		COMFORTABLE LIFESTYLE	
	Single	Couple	Single	Couple
Total per year	$24,250	$34,855	$43,665	$59,971

And it is not just retirees who are in the firing line as part of this welfare reform push. When Scott Morrison took on the Social Services portfolio in 2014 after a Cabinet reshuffle, he made his intentions very clear: 'Getting as many Australians as are able off welfare and into work will be one of my core goals.' Morrison would pass the social services baton to Turnbull government minister Christian Porter in late 2015. One of the pressing issues on Porter's mind was arresting the growth in payments made to recipients of the Disability Support Pension.

Like Morrison before him, Porter was incredulous that more than 800,000 Australians received the DSP. *The Australian*'s David Crowe pointed out the magnitude of the growth in expenditure in a November 2015 article titled '"More cuts needed" to fund new DSP programs, says Scott Morrison'.

Crowe said the cost of the DSP had swelled from $10 billion to $17 billion in the past decade, claiming it had outpaced inflation and other benchmarks linked to the country's working-age population.

'About 814,000 people received the DSP last year, down from 822,000 in June 2013,' he wrote. 'Even so, the DSP is the Commonwealth's fifth biggest program expense behind payments to the states ($57.7b), the Age Pension ($44.2b), Medicare services ($21.2b) and family tax benefits ($20.2b). Within four years, the DSP will surpass the FTB.'

The facts and figures are a stark reminder of just how hard it is to rein in welfare spending and achieve meaningful budget repair. In an October 2016 *Herald Sun* article titled 'Peta Credlin on how welfare dependence is ruining our economy', political adviser, commentator, and former Liberal Party chief of staff Peta Credlin depicts the challenge from another angle.

'... 80 per cent of all income taxes have to be ploughed back into social security payments. It explains why 40 per cent of all households get more back in benefits than they pay in tax – while the top 20 per cent of earners are slugged for 60 per cent of total income tax.

'... There are two issues here. First, the entitlement mindset – "my right" to be supported by the government; and second, the compassion mindset – the "community's obligation" to support people doing it tough.

'Well, sure, if there really is nothing you can do for yourself, the government has to step in.

'But governments that step in to help people who could and should be helping themselves weaken people's character and create a great deal of resentment among working families who hate being ripped off.'

Nobody takes kindly to giving up welfare benefits they have been receiving for some time. The tightrope the federal government is walking involves winding back social security spending and cutting the more obvious excesses from the system, while maintaining enough goodwill with enough of the electorate to survive a three-year election cycle.

The message to retirees, and those planning to retire, is clear: There is a direct link between the state of the nation's finances and the federal government's ability to continue funding social security benefits at the level that we, as a society, have become accustomed to. The money simply is not there.

As Andrew Bragg, Director of Policy & Research at Menzies Research Centre, pointed out in the *Australian Financial Review* on 3 January 2017, 'the tax-paying base is shrinking, and health and ageing costs are increasing.

'As debt approaches $350 billion, it is now clear successive governments made spending promises that couldn't be kept.

'... Existing and future promises will be worth even less unless there is a realistic reappraisal of the role of government as the population ages and we live ever longer.'

In a fiscal race to the bottom, one of Bragg's concluding observations is that, as a nation, we are now funding recurrent expenditure with borrowings – a state of affairs that simply would not be tolerated in any sustainable business setting.

This creates challenges for us all. Not only can we expect to live longer, but the government's ability to support us through old age is diminishing by the day.

This has led to a swathe of spending cuts – and one particularly memorable speech.

UNPOPULAR DECISIONS
IN THE NATIONAL INTEREST

'The age of entitlement is over, and the age of personal responsibility has begun.'

JOE HOCKEY

Joe Hockey may be remembered as one of our less popular treasurers. Although, to be fair, federal treasurers are rarely taken into the hearts of the Australian people. As Michael Kroger once remarked on Sky News, 'They make unpopular decisions in the national interest.'

Hockey came to office in September 2013 as Federal Treasurer in Tony Abbott's Coalition government. However, the seeds for his tumultuous tenure as the country's Chief Financial Officer were sewn some 18 months earlier.

In April 2012, Hockey travelled to the Institute of Economic Affairs in London to deliver a speech titled 'The end of the age of entitlement'. Much of the message was based in fact. Hockey's thesis – that governments had a responsibility to future generations to rein in welfare spending as a proportion of GDP – was perfectly reasonable.

'We cannot choose both higher entitlements and lower taxes. We must make a decision one way or the other,' he said.

'... The social contract between government and its citizens needs to be urgently and significantly redefined. The reality is that we cannot have greater government services and more government involvement in our lives coupled with significantly lower taxation.

'As a community, we need to redefine the responsibility of government and its citizens to provide for themselves, both during their working lives and into retirement.

'As part of this process, we must emphasise that government spending should be funded from revenue rather than by borrowing from future generations in whatever form that may take.

'... To be bold, I have some suggestions.

'The first is that people need to work longer before they access retirement benefits. When the Age Pension was introduced in Australia at age 65, life expectancy was 55. Today life expectancy is in the 80s.

'So you can understand how I was shocked to hear that one of the policy promises of one of the main French presidential election candidates, François Hollande, is to bring the official retirement age back down to 60 from 62.'

(In June 2012, just two months after Hockey's speech, François Hollande would indeed prevail in the French presidential election. And in a move that flew in the face of the austerity sentiment sweeping Europe at the time, he kept his promise to lower the retirement age from 62 to 60 – a decision his opponent described as 'madness'.)

Hockey concluded, 'The road back to fiscal sustainability will not be easy.

'It will involve reducing the provision of so-called free government services to those who feel they are entitled to receive them.

'It will involve reducing government spending to be lower than government revenue for a long time.

'... The political challenge will be to convince the electorate of the need for fiscal pain and to ensure that the burden is equally shared.'

The speech would come to symbolise Hockey's time as Treasurer. He was able to neatly articulate the long-term economic problems we need to solve as a nation, but failed to persuade enough of the Senate and the electorate that the Coalition's response was the best way forward – often on the grounds of unfairness. Or, as Hockey would later concede in his farewell speech to Parliament, 'The Abbott government was good at policy but struggled with politics.'

Many of Hockey's views made sense in the context of the Western world's post-GFC debt and deficit headwinds, but the narrative never landed with the electorate.

When he later delivered his first federal budget in May 2014, Hockey served up plenty of 'fiscal pain' (in the form of proposed spending cuts), but failed his own test of ensuring the 'burden is equally shared'. Spending cuts were widely seen to disproportionately affect people on lower incomes, and the proposed budget was written off by many commentators and voters as grossly unfair. Despite later arguing that 'the government had more courage than the Parliament', Hockey and the Coalition government fell short in making the case for such drastic budget measures. They failed to articulate how some of the harsher budget measures would ultimately pave the way for a brighter economic future in the medium term, so it was back to the drawing board and much of the proposed reform never saw the light of day.

In his article in *The Australian* on 17 May 2016, titled 'Federal election 2016: reformers knew how to sell policy', Troy Bramston contrasts the substantial budget reform achievements of the Hawke-Keating and Howard-Costello governments. He also laments the apparent inability of current politicians to make the case for transformational budget repair, and to take the electorate along on the journey in order to get the harder reforms through Parliament.

'Without higher growth, a bigger productivity dividend and improved competitiveness, we run the risk of the next generation being worse off than the present generation – something that has not happened in the post-war era,' he says.

'The kind of fiscal consolidation necessary for sustainable budget repair achieved under the Hawke-Keating and Howard-Costello governments are now artefacts from a bygone era. The political class is simply not capable of responding to this kind of challenge. Instead, the Coalition and Labor are promising to tax and spend more. This is the tragedy of this election campaign.'

Perhaps we also need to attribute at least some of the blame for this state of affairs to ourselves; the voting public. Partly because we created the gridlock in the Senate that makes legislation increasingly difficult to pass, and partly because we tend to collectively kick and scream at the mere suggestion of big bang reform.

As Tim Colebatch, Economics Editor of *The Age*, rightly points out in his article on 26 November 2013 titled 'We simply can't have our cake and eat it too', 'The common thread in all these issues is that events are moving far more rapidly than public opinion. And rather than use their positions of influence to persuade the public to catch up with reality, as Paul Keating did, the politicians are lining up with public opinion as if to defy it. That makes short-term sense, but also makes it impossible to tackle long-term challenges.'

Joe Hockey's experience in politics demonstrates the importance of language in the political debate. 'The end of the age of entitlement' was perhaps the right sentiment, but the choice of words was used against him and the Coalition time and again. That said, I suspect Hockey may take a degree of satisfaction from more recent welfare reforms that are underway – the latest attempts to meaningfully slow the rate of government expenditure growth. These measures are highly consistent with the ideas he floated in London back in 2012.

Since Hockey's infamous speech, welfare spending has become an increasingly delicate issue. The government's unenviable challenge is to contain welfare spending growth in order to achieve meaningful budget repair, while minimising the fallout at the ballot box.

But according to Ross Greenwood, the Nine Network's Business and Finance Editor, successive governments have struggled to strike this balance...

A NATION BUCKLING UNDER PRESSURE

*'Should any political party attempt to abolish
social security ... you would not hear of that party
again in our political history.'*

DWIGHT D. EISENHOWER

It is safe to say Ross Greenwood is a morning person. In addition to hosting a leading, nationally syndicated nightly radio program (on the political and financial issues of the day), he is up early to deliver the daily 'Money Minute' segment on the *Today* show with a missionary zeal. Greenwood has mastered the art of distilling complex financial and economic developments into a minute or two of accessible commentary and charts, which anyone can understand.

Following the global financial crisis, the political debate has been dominated by the deteriorating state of the nation's finances. Specifically, the unsustainable growth of our national debt, and promises about how and when the budget deficit, and overall level of debt, might ultimately improve.

Despite Australia achieving 26 years without a technical recession (between 1991 and 2017), the role of Federal Treasurer has not been an easy one to occupy since the Rudd government swept to power in 2007. Successive ministers have been hampered by uncontrollable factors like volatile iron ore prices and the inconvenient level of the

Australian dollar. At times, Wayne Swan, Joe Hockey and Scott Morrison have appeared bewildered by the scale and complexity of the fiscal challenge we confront as a nation, as they front the cameras to try to explain the gap between budget forecasts and reality. In a Senate as unpredictable as it is entertaining, coming up with workable reforms – which will contribute to meaningful budget repair – has been especially hard.

As discussed earlier, the Abbott government's proposed 2014 budget reforms were ambitious, and promised material improvement in the budget bottom line. However, perceptions of inequity were rife, the sales pitch was lacking, and, as a result, the public stopped listening. Commentators had a field day dissecting the reforms, and most concluded that the spending cuts were not distributed fairly. Writing for *The Guardian* in October 2015, economist, author, blogger and former public servant Greg Jericho summed up the public mood most succinctly: 'This wasn't good policy sold poorly; it was terrible policy sold worse.' The legislation would never satisfy the needs of a patchwork of crossbench Senators, and most of the proposed reforms were subsequently shelved.

This form of political gridlock frustrates Greenwood, who is all too aware of the dangers of the spiralling debt and deficit trend. As he pops up on the *Today* show to deliver his rapid-fire assessment of the federal government's more recent budget woes, he captures the conflict between a relatively brief three-year election cycle and the long-term fiscal reforms needed if we are going to ensure living standards for future generations are at least on par with ours. During his 'Money Minute' segment in April 2017, Greenwood said, 'Now there's the dilemma – politicians can't or won't cut welfare or pensions. It's too hard if you want people to vote for you, so the government has got to find other ways to get money.'

And the numbers are truly staggering. The figure that stands out in all of this is the sheer size of the spend on social security (including payments such as the Age Pension, Family Tax Benefit, Disability Support Pension and Newstart) as a proportion of total government spending. Despite the many publicised efforts to rein in expenditure, welfare spending is increasingly out of control. To date, the policy response has been insufficient to reverse, or even slow, the trend.

'The government this year is expected to spend $158 billion on social security or welfare. Well, that bill is due to rise to $191 billion within three years. So, in three years' time, the annual bill will be $33 billion bigger than it is today.'

Greenwood puts the dilemma into context by confirming that the welfare expenditure increase *alone* is equivalent to the total federal government spend on education ($33 billion per year), while defence spending pales in comparison at $27 billion per year. He points out that our national debt now stands at $317 billion, with an interest bill of some $12.3 billion per year. 'That's $33.9 million every day just in interest,' he laments.

A few hours later, on 2GB's *Ray Hadley Morning Show*, Greenwood gave a bleak assessment of the prospect of the Coalition government achieving any meaningful turnaround in the budget position.

'So, when we talk about getting the budget back into the black, between you and me, they haven't got a snowball's chance in hell of doing that,' he says.

'Because ultimately, when you go to work today, most of the money that you pay in taxes is going to go to someone else, in terms of social security and welfare. Now it doesn't go to education or it doesn't go to health, it doesn't go anywhere else. We can't balance the budget.

And when we can't balance the budget, we go to the credit card and we have to borrow more money, so the interest bill rises, and they're stuck... So they're too shy to tackle the very hard fundamental problem that is actually driving Australia closer to recession every day. That is the warning that's coming out of the Reserve Bank, that's the warning that's coming out of the bank regulators right now, and, ultimately, the politicians and largely the community are blind to it and doing not a damn thing about it.'

But for future generations, the prospect of a recession at some point in the short or medium term is the least of their worries. Just as there has never been more scrutiny on the federal budget and the path back to surplus (real or imagined), so too the issue of intergenerational equity has entered the debate.

In a 2005 *Loyola University Chicago Law Journal* article, titled 'Some Thoughts on Shortsightedness and Intergenerational Equity', Brett M. Frischmann refers to intergenerational equity as a 'principle of distributive justice. It concerns the relationship among past, present, and future generations.'

We often think about this concept through the lens of the notional responsibility each generation holds to ensure the next generation enjoys a higher standard of living. Frischmann argues that we have collectively become so short-sighted that we are failing to adequately consider the needs and wellbeing of our children and all future generations. This is as prevalent in discussions about the environment and our natural resources as it is in the realm of economics. Frischmann feels we should reconnect along the lines of the following compact:

'Each generation, in recognition of the blessings it receives and its duty of stewardship for posterity, ought to take into account explicitly and meaningfully the interests of future generations when making decisions that affect natural and communal resources.'

In 1965, then US President Lyndon Johnson said, 'If future generations are to remember us more with gratitude than with sorrow, we must achieve more than just the miracles of technology. We must also leave them a glimpse of the world as God really made it, not just as it looked when we got through with it.'

More than 50 years later, examples are emerging of countries that have taken steps to introduce structured parliamentary representation of future generations. In other words, politicians with a singular focus on making decisions in the best interests of future generations. The Finnish parliament has the Committee for the Future, while the Hungarian Parliamentary Commissioner for Future Generations was established in 2008 to 'reinforce advocacy for the natural environment and to safeguard intergenerational justice.'

Australian politicians might adopt a similar framework for weighing reform possibilities, which take into account the positive impact they may have over decades, rather than the bounce they may get in the polls in the context of a three-year electoral cycle. The problem in Australia right now is that the growth in welfare spending (in particular) is racing ahead. But as Greenwood points out, we are in a low-growth environment, so it is difficult to achieve a corresponding increase in government revenue via tax receipts ordinarily delivered by strong economic growth.

'The problem is [that] apart from the housing industry on the east coast of Australia, there's precious little growth in most industries, and government regulators are trying to slow down the housing markets,' he says.

'What you'd be better off doing is: guess what? Cutting your taxes, to individuals and to companies, and getting more people to work and more people off welfare. So cut that deal and maybe get a few more tax dollars through the door.'

Certainly, getting more people off welfare is becoming an increasingly important priority for the government. This will be achieved by encouraging people to remain in, or return to, some form of work.

What this means for people contemplating retirement in the short or medium term is that you should assume government financial assistance is likely to be less generous and harder to access as the years go by. This doesn't mean there won't be a reasonable safety net for the elderly and disabled members of society who most need support, but it does mean that, where you are considered to be of sufficient means, you are increasingly on your own. The country simply cannot afford the expenditure.

If social security benefits are likely to be less attractive over time, there are two remaining levers available to you to secure a comfortable lifestyle as you grow older: The amount you save and invest over your working life, and how long you remain employed for.

But what are the job prospects like for older Australians? All is revealed in Part 3.

PART 3

NAVIGATING
THE EVER-CHANGING
WORKPLACE

MEANINGFUL WORK MATTERS

*'The pitcher cries for water to carry
and a person for work that is real.'*

MARGE PIERCY

While longer life spans create funding challenges for individuals and governments, rising longevity also means you have decisions to make about how you are going to spend those additional years. A growing number of older Australians are choosing to spend some of their extra years working. The Australian Institute of Health and Welfare confirms that in March 2016, 13 per cent of over 65s were in work (or seeking work), and this has risen from 8 per cent in 2006.

Rudy Karsan, founder of US-based venture capital firm Karlani Capital, is a strong believer in the importance of doing meaningful work. In 2012, Karsan sold Kenexa, the human resources software company he founded and ran for 25 years, to IBM for $1.3 billon. Having achieved financial independence many times over, his reaction to achieving such a business milestone was unexpected.

Speaking during a May 2016 TEDx Talk at the University of Calgary, Karsan said, 'That should have been my crowning moment – the day the deal closed. It was the saddest day of my life. It took me months to recover and more than half those nights I fell asleep crying. It was hard. I had lost meaning.'

Meaningful work matters. More recently, Apple CEO Tim Cook was addressing students at the University of Glasgow, after receiving an honorary Doctorate of Science, when he said, 'My advice to all of you is, don't work for money – it will wear out fast, or you'll never make enough and you will never be happy, one or the other. You have to find the intersection of doing something you're passionate about and at the same time something that is in the service of other people. I would argue that, if you don't find that intersection, you're not going to be very happy in life.'

While Cook was talking to young graduates, his advice is just as relevant to any working person. If you have the opportunity to engage in meaningful roles in your 50s, 60s and 70s, this is likely to go a long way in determining the duration of your time in the workforce. Even Microsoft founder Bill Gates once told talk show host Larry King, 'Paul [Allen] and I, we never thought that we would make much money out of the thing. We just loved writing software.'

In other words, rather than working purely for financial reasons, work – and your inclination to continue working – takes on a different dimension when you have a sense of purpose about your job, and feel passionate about what you do each day.

In an April 2017 study conducted by Curtin University and consultancy firm Making Work Absolutely Human (mwah), titled 'Happy Workers: How satisfied are Australians at Work?', researchers found that the nature of the work you do is a far greater determinant of happiness than any financial reward.

Associate Professor Rebecca Cassells from Curtin Business School said the report highlights the working conditions that most commonly lead to greater job satisfaction.

'Australians who work for themselves or in small businesses, in the not-for-profit or government sector, and workers that can do some of their work from home each week, are more likely to be satisfied in their jobs,' she said.

More than 60 per cent of workers over 70 indicated they felt very satisfied with their job overall. This was much higher than Generation Y (24 per cent), Generation X (28 per cent), and even the baby boomer generation, where just 33 per cent reported high levels of job satisfaction. The difference is most likely due to the fact that many people working in their 70s are doing so for non-financial reasons. More likely, they are continuing a long career in an area of expertise they are passionate about, or they have consciously taken up a particular career later in life, in a role that is closely aligned to their sense of purpose. Both scenarios would tend to facilitate higher levels of job satisfaction.

On the issue of the importance of money in the job satisfaction equation, mwah CEO Rhonda Brighton-Hall says, 'It's what you do, how you are able to go about your work and who is alongside you that matters the most when it comes to job satisfaction ... Work is a core component of our existence, our identity, our financial independence, and ultimately, our overall wellbeing.'

While the Curtin University study focuses on the working conditions and scenarios that tend to be conducive to higher job satisfaction, there are also a number of intangible elements of our workplace experience that contribute to job satisfaction and the pursuit of meaning in our working lives. In a Foenander Public Lecture at The University of Melbourne, titled 'Meaningful Work in the 21st Century', Emeritus Professor Barbara Pocock, of the University of South Australia, identified four benefits of working that people enjoy, and that contribute to the level of meaning they derive from their career:

- A sense of efficacy, identity, contribution and/or vocation.
- The opportunity to learn.
- Social connection.
- Positive spillover into the home.

Pocock feels society's transition to more service-oriented and professional jobs increases the opportunities for workers to experience the positive elements of work. She also argues that given the increasing amount of time we spend at work, employers and governments have a vital role to play in ensuring more of us derive meaning from our jobs, stating, 'particular terms, conditions and contexts matter a great deal to the meaning we draw from work ... what the makers of these terms and conditions do – employers, unions and governments – can help make work more meaningful in lives that are increasingly shaped by the stamp of work.'

Your 50s and 60s provide the perfect opportunity to reflect on the work you have done during your career, and its alignment or otherwise to your individual values and purpose in life. In my experience, those who are engaged in meaningful work, which they are passionate about, tend to think they will continue to remain active in the workforce well into their 60s and possibly beyond – health permitting. Where they are fit and healthy, they are more likely to reject society's implied suggestion of retirement at age 60 or 65, and more likely to continue in their vocation, possibly at a decreasing level of intensity over time.

Those who are less engaged in their job for varying reasons, and those with lower job satisfaction, generally go down one of two paths. The first is embracing an earlier retirement, though this is largely dependent on their financial position and ability to fund their desired lifestyle without a regular pay cheque. The second is pursuit of a career change or reinvention, and this may involve a completely new career path, either by choice or necessity when a previous role ends.

In all scenarios, those fortunate enough to be involved in meaningful work – which remains important to them as they approach the traditional retirement age – enjoy higher levels of job satisfaction and more flexibility in the way they ultimately transition to life after work.

WHY OLDER AUSTRALIANS ARE PART OF THE SOLUTION

'You can retire from a job, but don't ever retire from making extremely useful contributions in life.'

STEPHEN COVEY

All too often, references to population ageing describe the demographic shift in negative terms. The proliferation of older Australians is frequently described as a 'problem' or a 'burden' on the economy, based on the outdated assumption that ageing is synonymous with the complete cessation of work, subsequent dependence on Centrelink benefits, and the absence of any further meaningful engagement in the workforce or contribution to the tax base.

The reality is that more than ever, older Australians are a significant and increasingly willing part of the solution to the financial challenges of an ageing population. Given the perilous state of the nation's finances, Australians need to remain in the workforce – in some capacity – for longer, before ultimately deciding to cease work altogether.

In the countless conversations I hold each year with older Australians, there is a noticeable trend away from the traditional notion of retirement at a predetermined point in time (age 60 or 65), and towards a more fulfilling and flexible progression, which may involve full-time or part-time work spanning an indefinite number of years – often well past age 65.

My regular conversations with pre-retirees reveal many different motivations for engaging in part-time work beyond the traditional retirement age, including the following:

- A preference for lifestyle flexibility, which allows for a balanced combination of work, family caring commitments, travel, hobbies and other community activities.

- Financial necessity whereby they may not yet feel they have adequate savings to allow them to stop working.

- A desire for regular social interaction.

- A need for ongoing mental stimulation and intellectual challenges.

- A desire to maintain structure and routine.

- A sense of identify and purpose.

- A continuing passion for a particular line of work or business.

- The sense that ceasing work simply feels unnatural or undesirable.

- Fear of boredom.

Wendy Thompson is one such example. When Wendy, in her late sixties, eventually retires from her career as a barrister, one of the first things she plans to do is turn the stories she tells her grandchildren into a series of books they can keep as a memento of their childhood. Comfortable with managing a demanding schedule, Wendy also has visions for a food and wine tourism business in Victoria's Yarra Valley.

But for now, she is focused on working on a number of cases in her highly successful work health and safety law practice.

Wendy is part of a trend of substantially higher participation rates among Australian workers aged 55-plus. Australian Bureau of Statistics data confirms the participation rate among 55-64 year-olds increased from 43 per cent in the early 1990s to 64 per cent in 2014. Meanwhile, 12 per cent of those aged 65-69 continue to work (up from 10 per cent).

Participation rate, people aged 55 and over by age group, 1984 - 2014

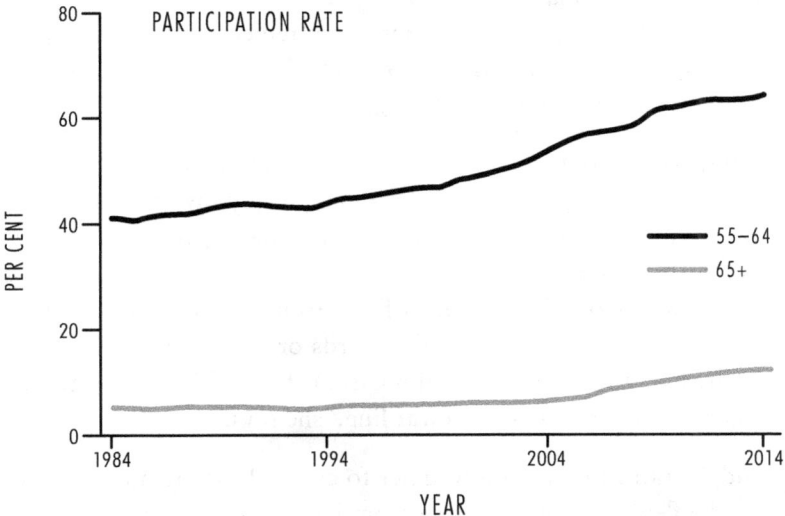

Source: Australian Bureau of Statistics, Australian Institute of Health and Welfare

Yet the motivations for working beyond the traditional retirement age of 65 are many and varied. For some, continuing on is due to financial necessity and the realisation that the amount you have saved will simply not deliver the lifestyle you desire when you cease work. It may also be that you still carry debt as the traditional retirement age approaches. Recent research from The Conversation found that between 1990 and 2013, the incidence of mortgage debt among those aged 55-64 more than tripled from 14 per cent to 44 per cent. Surging house prices in the eastern states have led to households taking on more debt, which is still being paid off as people hit their 50s and 60s.

Wendy is part of a group that continues to work predominantly for non-financial reasons. As a barrister specialising in work health and safety law, she is making the transition from full-time to part-time work as the first step towards eventual retirement. As we discuss her motivations for continuing to work into her late sixties, Wendy's passion for her career shines through.

'I think because of the nature of the work, I can honestly say I've not had one boring day at work. I thoroughly enjoy my work as a barrister. While it involves long hours and complex issues, the rewards I receive from working with other barristers, solicitors and clients from all walks of life make it difficult to move to full-time retirement. It is not just the financial rewards or the ability to work for oneself. It is the intellectual stimulation, friendship and collegiate life at the Bar that are most rewarding,' she says.

Wendy's transition has allowed her to continue to practice law, but with the flexibility of operating from her home in Sydney, or from her family retreat in Victoria's Yarra Valley.

'With benefits of technology, I can do advance work. I can read when I'm in Victoria as well as when I'm in New South Wales. So for that type of work, when I say transitioning, I'm transitioning out of more active court appearances. I will pass on to younger junior barristers smaller matters, and matters that require mentions and appearances for that sort of thing. I don't usually attend [court] myself for such matters unless it's unavoidable.'

In a world where increases to the retirement age are met with protest, Wendy's outlook is that age should not be the only determinant of whether someone should retire.

'Given the advances in medicine, I think 60 is far too young to have people retire because of age alone. I know that in legal firms and barristers' chambers, age is not a barrier to a person working. In many cases, it is preferred because of the experience of the person and their overall knowledge. There are also greater opportunities for the over-60s to start up their own consultancy business or other businesses.'

What, then, might ultimately trigger retirement?

'If there's any health reason, I would certainly bring forward any retirement plans. And of course, family issues, the health of your grandchildren or partner, and things like that would also weigh on that decision. But if things continue as they are at the moment, I would say I've probably got another three to five years to go.'

While there are many motivations for working past the traditional retirement age, many are willing to continue to work in some capacity provided two preconditions are met:

- Sufficient work opportunities are available – this is easier said than done, and is problematic for those in labour-intensive industries. There are far too many people over 60 who are willing and able to work, but unable to secure employment.

- Working conditions are flexible enough to allow them to work on their terms.

There is a lot riding on the creation of new employment opportunities for older Australians. The age of eligibility for the Age Pension is increasing to 67 (and could potentially go even higher), which means more people must stay in some form of employment for longer.

Unfortunately, the odds are stacked firmly against older jobseekers and employees, who are struggling to secure and retain decent jobs in a discriminatory and increasingly competitive work environment.

THE GREAT WORKPLACE DISCONNECT

'You are never too old to become younger.'

MAE WEST

The 2015 Intergenerational Report confirms that over-55s are the fastest growing cohort in Australia and will remain so for the foreseeable future. Within this demographic, an increasing number of older Australians are healthier and living longer than at any other time in history. They are willing and able to work well beyond the traditional retirement age, but the system is failing them in two ways.

First, too many employers still commit age discrimination, and many have not adapted their culture and organisational structure to take advantage of the skills and experience of older employees. Second, state and federal government incentive programs – designed to encourage more businesses to take on older employees – are simply not working.

The Restart Programme is a case in point. Launched with much fanfare in the 2014 federal budget, the scheme allocated $524 million to incentivise employers to employ more Australians over age 50. Employers can receive up to $10,000 over six months if they employ eligible mature-age jobseekers. Recipients need to be in receipt of social security benefits for at least six months prior to being eligible.

The expectation was that more than 30,000 new jobs would be offered to older Australians each year as a direct result of the scheme. Data on the success of government policies can be hard to come by when initiatives fail to live up to the sales pitch. However, in the first year of operation, only around 1,735 people were employed as a result of the program – a fraction of the target set by the federal government.

In April 2016, Attorney-General George Brandis asked the Australian Human Rights Commission to investigate the ways in which older people, and those with a disability, experience discrimination in Australia. The output was the 'Willing to Work' report, which found that of all the complaints made to the Australian Human Rights Commission by people aged over 45, around 71% were related to employment. Significantly, one-third of those who experienced age discrimination while looking for work gave up job hunting entirely. The report also found:

- In November 2015, the average duration of unemployment for mature-age individuals was 68 weeks (that's near enough to 16 months of job hunting), compared with 49 weeks for those aged 25-54 and 30 weeks for those aged 15-24.

- Australians aged 55 and over represent around a quarter of the population but only 16 per cent of the total workforce.

- Labour force participation declines with age. In November 2015, around 74 per cent of Australians aged 55-59 were participating in the workforce, compared to 57 per cent of those aged 60-64 and just 13 per cent of those aged 65 and over.

These statistics suggest age discrimination is deeply ingrained in the Australian workplace. As a result, older Australians routinely miss out on employment and workplace opportunities.

OPPORTUNITIES MISSED
IN THE WORKPLACE

'Old age hath yet his honour and his toil.'

ALFRED LORD TENNYSON

Dr Ruth Williams is a research fellow with the Centre for Workplace Leadership at The University of Melbourne. She is also the Academic Convenor at the Hallmark Ageing Research Initiative in the Melbourne School of Population and Global Health. She is an expert in workplace trends affecting older Australians, and a passionate advocate for 'positive ageing' and unlocking the value of mature-age employees. (The Australian Psychological Society describes positive ageing as 'the process of maintaining a positive attitude, feeling good about yourself, keeping fit and healthy, and engaging fully in life as you age.')

Williams has conducted significant studies into some of the potential benefits of remaining engaged in the workforce beyond the traditional retirement age.

'Anecdotally, I can't keep count of the number of people who have said, "I retired but I only lasted six months." People want to remain engaged. They get meaning out of life. It's very well documented that working actually increases health and wellbeing. Social contact is important and people get a lot out of it,' she says.

Such is the growing importance of the need for deeper insights into the societal implications of ageing that The University of Melbourne now offers a Master of Ageing on an online basis. 'As far as we are aware, we are the only course of our type in Australia. It's wholly online and it is multidisciplinary. It was driven by demand, and we've got architects, IT people and economists teaching design, technology and economics content with a focus on ageing.'

One of the recurring themes in my conversations with retirees, academics and business owners is that age discrimination is alive and well in Australian society, and there are strong views on the limitations such discrimination creates for older Australians. Williams has studied age discrimination in the workplace. She says that while things are improving, older workers still have trouble accessing the same opportunities as younger employees.

'There is still work to be done. Discrimination is rife within the recruitment stage. In the workplace, I think some employers still have stereotypical attitudes of older workers in the sense that they are stuck in their ways, and they don't want to undertake further learning and education opportunities. While that may be true, it's often that employers do buy into the stereotypes and have the assumptions that turn out to be incorrect.'

Williams points out that older workers can experience age discrimination in the workplace through lack of career advancement and job progression opportunities. She says some employers may invest less in their mature-age employees based on the outdated assumption that they're nearing retirement.

'A lot of employers think they're going to retire soon anyway. As we know, with the push to work longer, it could be that a 55-year-old has 10, 15, 20 years left in them in the workplace, and denying them of those career progressions – or learning, education and training opportunities – is doing a real disservice [to] the individual,' she says.

She also mentions more subtle age discrimination practices in the workplace, which might be intentional or unintentional. For example, perhaps older employees aren't invited out for drinks on a Friday night. Such a scenario is perhaps symbolic of a modern workplace that fails to integrate older workers into the organisation, and embrace the skills, experience and potential of mature-age employees.

In a March 2016 article in *The Sydney Morning Herald*, titled 'In the modern workplace, age 50 is considered old', executive coach Jenny Brice says, 'employers are reducing older workers from their workforce at alarming rates. Once older workers have left a job, it becomes difficult to re-enter the workforce. If they do, they are often underemployed and unable to maintain their previous standard of living ... Australians over the age of 50 do want to work. The issue is they often cannot get a job after their employment has been terminated. The new jobs they are offered are often casual or jobs that no one else wants.'

Frustrated by the level of age discrimination in the workplace, many older Australians are taking matters into their own hands and becoming self-employed. This has led to a new phenomenon: seniorpreneurship.

In an article published in Pursuit on 30 March 2016, titled 'Seniorpreneur: We need you', Williams explores the growth in older Australians starting their own businesses.

'... the "seniorpreneur" is proving to be the fastest growing segment of new business in Australia,' she states in her article. 'Almost 35 per cent of all new businesses are seniorpreneur start-ups.'

Williams questions whether this trend is driven more by a discovery of entrepreneurial zeal later in life, or more as a survival mechanism in the absence of sufficient employment opportunities.

'The trend seems to be that older people are one of the fastest growing groups that are starting their own enterprises. But I have a hypothesis that it is not necessarily driven by a cohort that finally want to be their own boss. Although they do have the financial capital to start something up, [and] they have the networks they have established over a lifetime career. They are in the perfect position, as opposed to young people, to start up and maintain the success of the start-up,' she says.

Figures show that an older jobseeker is likely to spend twice as long out of employment as a younger jobseeker. So if you leave a job or are made redundant in your 50s, it can be much harder to find your next job.

Williams says, 'I think the seniorpreneurs could definitely be driven by discriminatory practices whereby they can't get back into the workforce. Unfortunately, seniorpreneurship might not be all rosy, and is likely to be driven by need and desperation rather than entrepreneurial spirit.'

When asked about the government's role in creating job opportunities for mature-age workers, she struggles to find a positive.

'My understanding of the Restart Programme was that it was a sensational failure,' she says.

'Very few organisations took it up. There were a lot of barriers and red tape that prevented employers implementing the program. Larger organisations were thinking, "It's just too hard." And $10,000 to a company like Telstra? It was more trouble than it was worth.

'A similar program was rolled out in the UK and, again, it was a dismal failure. The proof of a pilot was there, yet the Australian government rolled it out anyway. It was doomed to fail, unfortunately.'

But is it really the role of government to incentivise employers to employ more mature-age workers? The very concept of subsiding companies to employ more older workers sends the message that such workers are a burden on organisations, when all the research indicates that the opposite is true.

'It's a very pessimistic kind of narrative. I think it should be driven by the market and sold as a business case benefit, emphasising the opportunity in employing older people. I think you need to highlight the success stories and I think it will pique the interest of organisations that might not already be on board,' says Williams.

A more sustainable answer is likely to come from the market, and from examples of businesses employing a higher number of older workers and thriving as a result.

One organisation leading the charge in this respect is Olderworkers. com.au, a Brisbane-based online job board, which has matched some 15,000 jobseekers with more than 1,000 employers nationwide.

INTRODUCING OLDERWORKERS.COM.AU

*'A man is not old until regrets
take the place of dreams.'*

JOHN BARRYMORE

Since April 2008, Judy Higgins and her husband Shane have made it their mission to help thousands of older Australians into employment.

Judy and Shane launched OlderWorkers after Shane's employer was acquired, and his role was affected by an organisational restructure. Shane was in his late 50s at the time, and his challenges were typical of the experiences he and Judy hear about from clients on a daily basis.

'The company I was working for was bought and almost all the older workers were moved sideways or retrenched. I was moved from a successful external sales role to being put on the phones. Humiliated and undervalued, after a short period, I resigned and found myself unemployed for almost two years. I would often get interviews, but would "just miss out", almost always on the basis of being over-qualified,' Shane says.

Using this experience as motivation, Shane and Judy have grown their business rapidly, based on a deep understanding of the needs of older workers, and the creation of a job-hunting environment where age is not considered a disadvantage.

When asked about the effectiveness of government incentives like the Restart Programme, Judy is less than complimentary.

'They are totally ineffective. There is only one incentive for employers to employ mature-age jobseekers – Restart. And since it was implemented (in 2014), we have had one query. Put simply, it has not worked ... Research will show that federal and state employment incentives for a variety of cohorts don't work,' she says.

Despite the success the Higgins have achieved in matching employers and older employees via Olderworkers.com.au, Judy is frustrated at the age discrimination that is still very much evident in the employment market.

'It hasn't improved ... "Willing to Work" confirms that age discrimination is rife. In an employment environment that favours employers, the situation has become worse instead of better and we don't expect this will change anytime soon.'

Judy believes age discrimination often presents in subtle ways, though she notes that some employers will openly say they are looking for younger workers for particular roles. Pet peeves of the jobseekers she works with include not hearing back from employers after sending a job application, and a lack of respect and acknowledgement from employers about the skills older workers bring to the table. 'They are often made to feel worthless in their job hunting,' she says.

Fortunately, not all companies are dismissive of the contribution older employees can make to their success. In fact, an increasing number of companies are bucking the trend entirely, with a *preference* for older workers.

FINDING AN AGE-FRIENDLY EMPLOYER

'Experience achieves more with less energy and time.'

BERNARD BARUCH

Judy interacts with employers across a wide range of industries. She counts a number of major companies – including Woolworths, Commonwealth Bank, Allianz, Coles, Bupa and Bunnings – as clients who advertise roles specifically for older Australians on her job board.

Judy cites an array of benefits to those employers, including sourcing older employees who will generally stay in a job longer than their younger counterparts, and thereby reduce recruitment and training costs.

'They have diverse life experience to bring to the workplace, they have high-level problem-solving skills, and often take on informal mentoring roles. They bring job skill levels that they willingly and sometimes unwittingly pass on to younger colleagues,' she says.

She believes smart organisations are beginning to realise the need to ensure their staffing mix is more consistent with their client profile.

Ruth Williams is in agreement.

'Some organisations are quite desperate to keep older workers because of the particular knowledge they hold,' she says.

'For example, in the mining industry, the older workers have specific knowledge to operate specific machines or specific technology that was around when they were in their peak career. That technology has either evolved or is being replaced. I have heard that they are getting older workers back to operate this equipment, for example. That they have this specific knowledge that nobody else seems to have. They are literally bending over backwards to keep older workers in the workforce.'

Williams pinpoints Bunnings as another good example of a company that is unlocking the value of older workers.

'Bunnings are very well known for their older workforce. I think their model is sensational. Who better to buy some electrical equipment from than an ex-tradesman? Buy paint from an ex-painter. It's a perfect scenario that's been brilliant for Bunnings,' she says.

She also mentions the major banks, which recognise that many older people still prefer to visit a branch and speak to a teller, rather than using online channels or an ATM. As a result of this, there is a more conscious effort among the big banks to employ older tellers who better match their customer base.

And it seems parts of the hospitality industry may be thinking along similar lines.

'A lot of the hotels like Accor are doing the same where they are hiring older workers to greet the largely growing cohort of travellers, which are the silver-haired, cashed-up retirees,' Williams says.

Still, Williams feels there is a long way to go if employers are to fully harness the workplace potential of older Australians.

'I think HR managers might need to think outside the square a bit on this one,' she says.

Ultimately though, as more companies begin to recognise the value of mature-age workers, the onus is on older jobseekers to present themselves in the best light possible. This is where social media plays an increasingly important role.

HOW SOCIAL MEDIA CAN BOOST YOUR JOB PROSPECTS

'Social media presents an opportunity for business people to connect and know each other prior to a phone call or email taking place.'

JEFFREY GITOMER

Talk to most business owners, and it is more than likely they will nominate the attraction of quality employees as the most critical prerequisite for the success of their business. Choosing the wrong employees leads to expensive recruitment and retraining costs, which disrupt workplace culture and impede business growth, while depleting financial resources.

Historically, the recruitment process has relied heavily on a job candidate's résumé, the interview process, perhaps a psychometric test, and a handful of referees (carefully selected by the candidate). This provides a limited window into a candidate's true suitability, mainly because the candidate is able to manage the portrayal of their suitability at each stage of the recruitment process (by emphasising the most favourable information, while omitting any less favourable information).

But Fiona McLean is seeking to change that.

McLean is a Sydney-based HR executive and founder of The Social Index, an online start-up revolutionising the way companies recruit and select new staff. McLean launched The Social Index in August 2016 to provide employers with deeper insights into the digital footprint of candidates applying for jobs. In doing so, employers are better equipped to make the right recruitment decisions.

With more than 20 years' experience as an HR executive in Sydney and London, in some of the world's largest financial institutions, McLean had a growing sense that more useful tools were needed to determine the intangible characteristics of job candidates, such as reputation, character, level of influence, and effectiveness of networking.

The rise of social media means we are all leaving behind a growing collection of digital 'evidence', which can be mined and analysed, and potentially offer employers and recruitment companies valuable insights into your suitability or otherwise for a particular role. Recognising that these masses of data accumulating on social media platforms had the potential to become a valuable tool in the recruitment process, McLean spent more than three years planning and developing a unique diagnostic tool, which can accurately aggregate and analyse a candidate's digital footprint to determine their personal brand, the frequency of their social media activity, their potential 'reach' and 'fit', and, perhaps most importantly, their alignment or otherwise to a company's brand, culture and values.

In a recent conversation, McLean explains the power individuals now have to promote and manage their professional reputation via social media.

'The emergence and now dominance of social media in the workplace means that this ability to develop and credential a reputation is in the hands of every employee, regardless of level and tenure. So we developed our platform to help businesses, and individuals, navigate this new reputation-focused workplace. Our platform helps businesses make sure you have the best candidate by understanding how their reputation aligns to their culture and brand, and for individuals gives them a better way to manage, credential and showcase your key skills, network, industry fit and other relevant attributes for the role,' she says.

In an August 2016 interview with Chris Pash of Business Insider, 'An inside look at the tool employers will soon use to check your social media profile', McLean discusses the power of The Social Index in enabling employers to make better hiring decisions.

'I wanted to solve the problem of how to know that a great candidate is really a great culture fit for a company,' she says. 'So we created a data-driven platform that could help businesses understand the relevance of social media in the context of their workplace.'

During the recruitment process, candidates receive a link to provide their approval for The Social Index to conduct the data analytics process. Importantly, privacy protocols are robust, so employers don't have access to individual social media posts. Based on the output of a proprietary algorithm (generated with the candidate's permission), employers and individuals using The Social Index are presented with an infographic report, which distils data from a wide range of popular social media platforms into a practical summary of a candidate's digital footprint. The information is an enormous help to recruitment companies and HR professionals, as it provides them with another valuable reference point to prioritise candidates based on their relative suitability.

Even without The Social Index, you get the sense that informal Google searches are now commonplace for recruiters and HR professionals seeking to gain a more rounded view of potential job candidates. McLean suggests that 93 per cent of recruiters are likely to look at a candidate's social media profile, and 42 per cent have reconsidered a candidate – either positively or negatively – after doing so. It's also worth noting that 98 per cent of employees use at least one social media site for personal use, with 50 per cent posting about their employer.

Jobseekers of all ages should take note. When it comes to how attractive you are to a potential employer, what you do and say on social media matters more than ever. The topics you discuss, and the frequency and nature of your social media contributions, are under the spotlight. They could be the difference between landing that dream job and just missing out.

In a recent blog post on The Social Index web site, McLean says, 'Because social media is so easy for employers to find, it can make or break employment opportunities. Employers often have a very easy time finding and accessing social media accounts, and they often find them without your knowledge and use them to decide if you're an employable candidate. That means that a single inappropriate "selfie" could prevent you from getting the job of your dreams.'

It is yet another consideration as you navigate the modern workplace. If it all sounds a bit daunting, McLean says you can use your social media profile to differentiate yourself in a positive way.

'These new social media platforms are designed to make it easy for anyone to use, regardless of technical skills,' she says. 'Smart decision-making and an "employment-ready" social media account can actually help your chances, and possibly make it easier to beat your competition.'

Of course, an employment-ready social media account isn't the only thing you need to consider when searching for a job.

McLean says, 'Leverage your network, connect with recruiters and connect directly with companies via social media. Older employees are in a strong position to leverage their network and not just with former colleagues (who may be in the same position!), but those friends and connections from weekend activities, church, art, sport, or other community-related activities who may know of an upcoming position or can put you in contact with a key decision-maker. Leveraging the wider network is one of the most powerful ways to get a job.'

If you're an older jobseeker struggling to find work, Judy Higgins says there are ways to increase your probability of success in the employment market. She encourages her clients to focus on the following:

- Ensure you have an up-to-date, contemporary CV. It will be your first impression on a potential employer, so you want it to look impressive.

- Look at new and emerging industries where you may have an interest or skills, and where there are jobs available.

- Keep an open mind about training. Is there a particular course that would help you acquire new skills in industries and locations where there are jobs available?

- Craft each job application individually. Employers can smell generic applications from 400 paces, and it is not a good first impression.

- Research the company you are applying to, and know as much as you can about that company to ensure you are a good fit.

- Make sure you understand the details of the job you are applying for. How can you prepare a good application if you don't know what the job is about?

- Consider doing some volunteering in areas that utilise existing skills and teach new skills.

Remember, it is easier to get a job when you have a job. Don't be too picky – the 'perfect job' just might not exist.

Of course, employment is not the only way to fund your retirement years. Another way to grow your nest egg is via savings and investments. But this, too, has its own set of challenges, discussed in detail in Part 4.

PART 4

PLANNING FOR
YOUR FINANCIAL FUTURE
IN A WORLD OBSESSED
WITH 'NOW'

THE RETIREMENT PLANNING CHALLENGE

'To be an investor you must be a believer in a better tomorrow.'

BENJAMIN GRAHAM

These days, the financial challenge of retirement planning is funding a 25 to 30-year period, and for many people this is a daunting task. In 2014, even the architect of the superannuation system, former Prime Minister Paul Keating, argued that working for 30 or 35 years to build up your super through compulsory contributions (currently 9.5 per cent of your salary) is probably not going to be enough to allow you to sustain a comfortable, potentially 30-year retirement. This is particularly the case for those approaching retirement today, who have not had the benefit of a full career supported by compulsory super contributions. When introduced in 1992, the rate of compulsory super was set at three per cent of your salary, and has only gradually increased to the current level of 9.5 per cent.

Keating's view is that the super system was set up based on life expectancy in the 1980s, and this means it was designed to help people supplement their retirement income between ages 60 and 80. What has happened since, of course, is that average life expectancy has continued to march higher. It is now far more common for people to live well into their 80s and 90s – in some cases by quite some measure. In a May 2014 *Lateline* interview with the ABC's Tony

Jones, Keating said life expectancy trends have left the superannuation system behind.

'So, we have superannuation mach one, the one I set up, which is 60 to 80, and we have now nothing in respect of superannuation mach two, which is 80 to 100. At the moment, nearly all of those people would rely on the pension because their superannuation lump sum will have well and truly expired by the time they touch 80.'

In a June 2014 report titled 'Adequacy and the Australian Superannuation System', Deloitte concluded that despite the projected growth in the superannuation system over the next 20 years, our collective savings will still fall well short of providing a comfortable retirement for most retirees. The rate at which life expectancies have increased has left the super system under pressure to deliver on its original objectives to take pressure off Age Pension expenditure and enable a more comfortable retirement for more Australians. Deloitte's starting position is that unless Australians are prepared to work longer or contribute more (ideally both), then it is unlikely most would build their super to sufficiently support a comfortable retirement.

The report grimly stated, 'Have no doubt, superannuation balances for the overwhelming majority of Australians retiring in the next few years will be nowhere near sufficient to provide even a modest retirement lifestyle – let alone a comfortable one … It appears that, 25 years on from the introduction of [the Superannuation Guarantee], we are still well short of meeting the needs of retiring Australians.'

In proposing solutions, Deloitte suggests Australians need to become better educated and informed in order to respond to the challenges of retirement planning in the 21st century. This means accepting that the current level of compulsory super is unlikely to be enough for many. It also means proactively planning for retirement and ensuring your plans evolve as you get older – particularly during periods where you have more disposable income (this is typically in the later stages of your career).

In his interview with *Lateline*, Keating proposed a longevity levy to fund Australians who live beyond age 80, which would be an additional tax on the population to ensure money was set aside specifically to assist people in funding their expenses once they get well into old age.

In the absence of such a levy, there are really three levers available to you to ensure your money goes the distance in retirement. First, you can start saving earlier for your long-term retirement needs. Intuitively, it makes sense to start saving for retirement from a younger age. But of course, long-term savings are just one priority competing with more pressing shorter term commitments – such as mortgage repayments and children's education – in your 30s, 40s and 50s.

Second, you can save at a higher rate. Where cash flow allows, salary sacrifice contributions are a powerful way to bridge the retirement funding gap, and achieve tax benefits and greater compounding of returns. The rate at which compulsory superannuation contributions are made on your behalf can also have a major bearing on how much you end up with in retirement. The Superannuation Guarantee is frozen at 9.5 per cent, yet the original intent of the super system was to progressively increase the rate to be much higher. Keating said, 'Nine per cent is not enough to get you a replacement rate of 70 to 75 per cent. It has to be 12 per cent – at least 12. You remember in the 1995 budget, I had it going to 15.'

The third lever you can pull to boost your retirement savings is to work longer. The dual benefit of working longer is that every additional year you work is one extra year of money saved and one less year of money drawn down from your savings. The combination has a powerful effect on the longevity of your capital when you do decide to retire. So, when you ultimately decide to stop working, you've done your future self a favour by remaining in the workforce (provided those opportunities are available to you).

WHY YOU
ARE INCREASINGLY
ON YOUR OWN

'Retirement is the ugliest word in the language.'

ERNEST HEMINGWAY

While we are all encouraged to save diligently to achieve a self-funded retirement, the reality is that many Australian retirees live on some combination of a part or full Age Pension, as well as their own private savings (usually superannuation assets and other investments such as shares, property and cash). This is a fairly common set-up for a large number of retirees in Australia.

According to the Australian Institute of Health and Welfare, more than 80 per cent of Australians aged over 65 rely on some form of Age Pension to meet their ongoing income needs in retirement. The problem is that this source of income is becoming increasingly inaccessible. As you know, the federal government is determined to limit the growth in welfare spending. January 2017 is the perfect example of widespread cuts, which saw some 320,000 Australian retirees lose some or all of their part Age Pension benefit.

These cuts saw some couples lose up to around $15,000 per year in Age Pension payments, while singles lost up to $9,000 a year.

If you're a couple trying to live on $50,000 or $60,000 a year, and

$15,000 of that is no longer available to you, then you'll need to draw down on your savings in a more substantial way to continue to meet your living expenses. Make no mistake – that was the government's very intention in altering the Age Pension assets test so drastically. As the changes took effect, it took the view that if you're a couple with more than $816,000 in assets, in addition to your family home, then you can do without part Age Pension support. Singles with more than $542,500 were sent the same message – if the government of the day deems that you are of sufficient means, then you are on your own.

Families affected by these cuts had a choice – live on less, or draw more from their existing financial resources. Some responded by altering their investment strategy in pursuit of higher income. An understandable response, though caution is needed, as any pursuit of a higher level of income is often accompanied by additional investment risk, which can put your capital in jeopardy.

The key lesson here is the importance of doing the numbers and working out how much you will eventually need to live comfortably when you reach retirement.

As the government becomes increasingly determined to cut welfare spending, you need to focus on the level of assets you are building up in your own right. The more you accumulate, the less dependent you will ultimately be on social security payments, which are becoming less certain – and more meagre – by the day.

BUT HOW MUCH IS ENOUGH?

'Investing should be like watching paint
dry or watching grass grow.If you want excitement ...
go to Las Vegas.'

PAUL SAMUELSON

If we look at the state of retirement preparedness in Australia, some concerning statistics emerge. Countless studies have shown that many Australians approaching traditional retirement age simply will not have enough saved and therefore will not be able to achieve the level of comfort they aspire to. The result for many will be the need to make more sacrifices, and the prospect of less lifestyle choices, while some will need to continue working, irrespective of the level of enjoyment and satisfaction they derive from their career.

A July 2017 survey of 45-84 year-olds conducted by Australian Unity and Empirica found that almost 30 per cent of pre-retirees did not feel they would be in a comfortable position at retirement, while 77 per cent of 45-64 year-olds had not begun formally planning for their retirement. Australian Unity Wealth CEO, David Bryant, said the national survey explored retirement preparedness, while providing insights into common financial concerns and attitudes towards the future.

He said, 'Worryingly, the data shows more than three-quarters of 45-64 year-olds are running blind. They're neglecting to get advice, not proactive about planning and a good majority have no idea about the recent government [super] changes. What's clear is that many baby boomers – though reliant on super for their retirement, don't understand it, and don't have a plan for their retirement beyond it.'

A closer look at the research reveals some telling statistics about the level of preparation Australians undertake for life after work:

- Only 30 per cent of pre-retirees said that they were making extra contributions to their superannuation (despite assuming on average that 52 per cent of their post-retirement income will come from their super).

- 47 per cent of pre-retirees said they hold no investments apart from their super.

- 44 per cent of pre-retirees described themselves as 'not proactive' when it comes to their retirement.

- 58 per cent of pre-retirees do not believe they have enough in super to retire without accessing the Age Pension.

- 27 per cent of pre-retirees said they are 'very' or 'extremely' worried about having enough money to retire on.

- 29 per cent of pre-retirees disagreed or strongly disagreed that they will be in a comfortable position when they retire.

Those surveyed who had already retired had some simple but highly practical advice for those who are currently planning their retirement. Their top five tips? Plan ahead, clear debts, spend sensibly, invest wisely, stay healthy.

Such studies are a dime a dozen, and most arrive at a similar conclusion. For example, a 2014 MLC Retirement Survey of 2,000 Australians found more than half of those surveyed expected they would not have enough money to retire on. Around 32 per cent expected a large financial shortfall, while 25 per cent expected a shortfall to a lesser extent. The research found just 3.5 per cent of Australians thought they would have more than enough money to ensure they could continue the lifestyle they had become accustomed to.

The main barriers identified to saving enough were major health problems, loss of employment, and lack of a formal investment plan. Divorcees expected the largest financial shortfall when they reached retirement, while professionals and those earning more than $100,000 per year were (not surprisingly) most comfortable with their retirement prospects.

There is also a mismatch between the expectations of those planning for retirement and the reality.

Galaxy Research conducted in 2013 (commissioned by Sunsuper) found many Australians have unrealistic expectations about how much it will cost to achieve the lifestyle they desire in retirement. The survey of more than 1,500 Australians found many believed that an income of $3,700 per month ($44,400 per year) would be sufficient for a comfortable retirement.

Sunsuper General Manager Steven Travis said, 'Australians are disconnected with what it costs to fund a retirement. They don't really know what retirement costs and they've never really costed what they would need.'

So how much is enough? The ASFA Retirement Standard is a benchmark that measures just this. By making estimates of the average household spend on various items, the benchmark provides a handy reference point when trying to figure out how much you are likely to spend when you retire.

For example, in March 2017, ASFA suggested a couple needed $59,971 per year for a comfortable lifestyle, or $34,855 for a modest lifestyle. Meanwhile, individuals required $43,665 per year to be comfortable, or $24,250 for a modest lifestyle. The ASFA Retirement Standard describes a comfortable retirement as enabling an older, healthy retiree to be involved in a broad range of leisure and recreational activities, and to have a good standard of living through the purchase of such things as household goods, private health insurance, a reasonable car, good clothes, a range of electronic equipment, and domestic and occasionally international holiday travel. Conversely, a modest retirement is considered better than the Age Pension, but still only allows for fairly basic activities.

For context, a couple receiving the full Age Pension in June 2017 receives $34,819 per year, while an individual receives $23,096 per year.

Of course, terms like 'comfortable' and 'modest' are highly subjective, and will differ vastly for everyone. Some will spend considerably more in retirement, while others may be more frugal and not need quite so much – we are all different. Such benchmarks are constructed using a detailed breakdown of average expenditure on a range of household items for retirees. While the ASFA Retirement Standard is a good starting point for assessing how much money you may need based on the lifestyle you would like to lead, there is no substitute for doing your own budget and coming up with an estimate of how much your household needs to be comfortable.

Once you have a figure to work with, you can begin to understand the level of savings you will need to accumulate to be able to achieve your desired lifestyle in retirement. Again, the ASFA Retirement Standard is a useful guide in arriving at a figure. For example, the combined superannuation balance a couple will need to achieve a comfortable income of $59,971 per year is estimated at $640,000, while individuals are likely to need $545,000 to ensure they can achieve an income of at least $43,665 per year in retirement. (Figures are based on the means test for the Age Pension as at 1 January 2017, and assume CPI at 2.75 per cent and average investment earnings of 6 per cent per annum).

If your aim is a 'modest' retirement, ASFA estimates couples will need just $35,000 in savings to supplement the Age Pension while singles will need $50,000.

However, there are major challenges associated with saving and investing – particularly in today's fast-paced, noisy world.

INSTANT GRATIFICATION
AND THE PSYCHOLOGY OF MONEY

*'The four most dangerous words in investing are:
this time it's different.'*

JOHN TEMPLETON

Why is it that so many Australians feel unprepared for retirement, despite the fact that we have a growing retirement savings system that is the envy of the world? It turns out the answer may be staring us in the face. We are not necessarily wired to make the best investment decisions, and sometimes we can be our own worst enemy when trying to grow our wealth.

Simon Russell is better equipped than most to make sound financial decisions in today's increasingly noisy investment environment. With a diverse professional background spanning psychology, asset consulting and investment banking, Simon is an author and Director of Behavioural Finance Australia, a successful consultancy combining his background in psychology with his skills in the financial services sector. He provides consulting services to financial institutions, super funds, financial adviser groups and other investors to help them better understand the psychology of markets and decision-making, and thus make better investment choices.

Russell nominates 'short-termism' as one of the most significant mental challenges preventing you from making better decisions in the long run.

'It makes a lot of sense. We live in the present day and all the stimulus, and everything about today, is vivid. I can see things, I can feel them, I can touch them, and I have emotional responses to them,' he says. 'But everything about the future is the opposite. It becomes abstract, it becomes harder to visualise, and I can't experience an emotional connection.'

In a discussion with Russell about his book, *Applying Behavioural Finance in Australia*, he relayed the details of a famous study on the topic of delayed gratification by psychologist Walter Mischel. The Stanford marshmallow experiment, conducted in the late 60s and early 70s, involved children who were offered a choice between one marshmallow offered immediately, or two marshmallows (or some other treat) offered 10 to 15 minutes later. The study later followed these children through life, and the research concluded that the children who were able to resist the offer of a single marshmallow – and hold out for a longer period in order to receive two marshmallows – tended to achieve higher outcomes on a range of measures, including high school grades, body mass index, and propensity to go on to higher education. Even at that early age, having the psychological self-control to delay gratification can be a powerful indicator of your future behaviour and success in life.

Instant gratification is the thread that runs through the fabric of our on-demand existence. It is the ultimate form of short-termism. We are so focused on the here and now that we find it extraordinarily difficult to visualise the distant future, much less make decisions that may be in the interests of our future selves. The realm of finance is a perfect example of this. Simon Russell's research indicates that we struggle to form an emotional connection to our future selves – to the point where that person seems like a stranger. 'Why would I save for this stranger in the future? This doesn't even seem like me, and I can't imagine what it is going to be like to be 70 or 80,' he says.

So the first challenge is that we're asked to think and plan decades in advance, when we are wired to focus very much on the short term, and outcomes in the here and now. That is not an easy conflict to resolve.

THE PERILS OF SHORT-TERMISM

'Much success can be attributed to inactivity.
Most investors cannot resist the temptation
to constantly buy and sell.'

WARREN BUFFETT

The more you scan society for further examples of short-termism, the more you uncover. A three-year electoral cycle encourages politicians to focus disproportionately on winning the next election at all costs; the focus is on election promises, rather than reforms that may take time to implement, but deliver benefits over decades. Listed companies are under pressure from analysts to hit half-yearly profit targets, despite the need to make strategic decisions to achieve growth over the long term. Even employee behaviour is easily skewed by bonus and performance management structures, which reward near-term milestones over worthwhile projects that may take years to bear fruit. The system is set up to foster a disproportionate focus on short-term outcomes, and the opportunity cost is lost in the rush.

TRUMP, MINI-CRISES AND MEDIA SENSATIONALISM

The Brexit vote and Donald Trump's US presidential election win are classic examples of extreme market noise based on major political developments, which probably led to a lot of kneejerk reactions and unfortunate investment decisions.

It remains to be seen what the long-term implications of those developments will be. However, the markets took both decisions in their stride, with many observers surprised by the strong performance of global stock markets in the wake of these events. Prior to the US election, many people believed a Trump victory would be a negative for shares due to Trump's lack of political experience, the unpredictability of his political agenda, and the perceived relative safety of a Clinton administration.

It is extraordinary, then, that on the night of his election victory, as Trump delivered an unexpectedly conciliatory victory speech, US share market futures bounced aggressively. When markets opened the next morning, both the Dow Jones Industrial Index and the S&P 500 soared.

What had happened? Perhaps in the wake of the unexpected result, investors had – for the first time – looked more closely at Trump's economic policies, and formed the view that, in the short term at least, they would boost US economic growth and corporate profitability.

Events like Brexit and Trump's victory, and other much-hyped events such as the Greek debt crisis and the US fiscal cliff, are sometimes referred to in the media as 'mini-crises'.

According to Philippe Jordan, CEO of Capital Fund Management, research by the OECD claims there has been something like 400 of these 'mini-crises' over the last 55 years. On average, that's one mini-crisis every eight weeks! These events are occurring far more frequently than you realise, and therefore affecting the investment decisions you make. As each mini-crisis unfolds, investors are inclined to make kneejerk reactions. However, these reactions can hinder any attempts at long-term wealth creation.

Jordan's advice?

'Crisis is a form of entertainment,' he says. 'You open the newspaper and read about crises and it's entertaining because our business is pretty dry ... The energy that we spend as a community on whether this time is different than last time is a colossal dissipation of resources.

'Forget the drama. Forget the sense of exceptionalism that we want to have intimately in our lives.'

Jordan describes market noise as 'a huge distraction from what we really need to be paying attention to, which is very basic stuff and we all know it.'

In an August 2016 interview with *Investor Daily*, he said, 'We know just by looking at the past that crisis is the de facto operating code of markets and societies in general. They are not the exception, they are the norm ... But there are hundreds of pseudo-crises that you're supposed to do something about, and doing something about them is precisely the wrong thing to do.'

Graham Rich is a pioneer of the funds management research industry in Australia, having brought the Morningstar business to the local market in 1997. These days, he is Managing Partner and Dean of the PortfolioConstruction Forum, a leading specialist provider of ongoing investment education and certification for portfolio construction practitioners.

In August 2016, Rich delivered the opening address of the Portfo-lioConstruction conference (themed 'The long and short of it') at Australian Technology Park, attended by investment professionals and experts from Australia and around the globe.

On stage, Rich held an extraordinarily well-behaved 18-month-old boy (Sebastian) to challenge the audience to think about the true defi-nition of investing for the long term for the benefit of young Sebas-tian's generation. He challenged the audience to consider the intergen-erational equity challenges we face as a society – the idea that each generation should enjoy a higher standard of living than the last.

'Don't you reckon it's intriguing,' he begins, 'that a challenge we all face is this paradox between thinking about the long term and the constant challenge of thinking about the now? Sebastian is growing up in a world where there is more stuff going on immediately, chal-lenging us to think about right now. Challenging us to think about high frequency trading, social media, the 24/7 news cycle, all the stuff that keeps this friction between the long term and the short term.'

In a more recent interview I conducted with Rich, he argued that concerns over the impact of short-termism are not necessarily new, and that, throughout history, societal and technological advance-ment has often been accompanied by fears that people will be dis-tracted from longer term priorities.

'After all, it's human nature for most of us to think about the here and now more than the past or the long-term future,' he says. 'How-ever, the accelerated growth of interconnectedness in recent years – further fuelled by the internet – certainly appears to have heightened the focus on short-term issues.

'Addressing these issues is particularly important when put into con-text of how our market-driven democracy puts the primary onus of responsibility for retirement income onto each individual. In other words, there is a government expectation that individuals will plan for their own long-term financial wellbeing, notwithstanding that this is counterproductive to how many of us think and behave. On top of all of this is the challenge of thinking about intergenerational equity (which fails with excessive short-termism), and of social justice for those less fortunate in our communities who just cannot make effective plans for their long-term futures. So, concerns over excessive short-term behaviour by otherwise responsible individuals are valid and real.'

RETIREMENT TRENDS AND TRANSITIONS

'The pessimist complains about the wind; the optimist expects it to change; the realist adjusts the sails.'

WILLIAM ARTHUR WARD

If short-termism is one of the reasons for the lack of retirement preparedness, how is retirement actually playing out today? And what can you learn from the experiences of current retirees as they transition from the workforce?

A good place to start is the 2017 HSBC study I referred to in Part 2, titled 'The Future of Retirement: Shifting Sands'. The study is based on a global survey of more than 18,000 people in 16 countries, including 1,000 Australians. The report explores the way the ageing population, rising healthcare costs, and record low interest rates are affecting the retirement plans of people around the world.

Here are some of the key findings of the working-age people surveyed:

- 58 per cent say they will continue working to some extent in retirement.

- 50 per cent think low interest rates means they will need to work for longer.

- 66 per cent believe levels of national debt mean there will be less support for the elderly.

- 77 per cent believe retirees will have to spend more on healthcare costs in the future.

- 68 per cent are concerned about the impact of economic uncertainty on their ability to save for retirement.

- 70 per cent would be willing to defer their retirement for two years or more to have a better retirement income.

- 21 per cent of the Australians surveyed think they will be financially comfortable in retirement, based on how their retirement saving is progressing.

When respondents were asked about the best financial advice they had received in an earlier HSBC Future of Retirement study, *Life After Work*, the most common answers included:

- Start saving at an early age.

- Don't spend what you don't have.

- Buy your own home as soon as you can afford to.

- Start saving a small amount regularly.

- Develop a financial plan for the future.

Individually, these ideas represent a practical list of good habits. But if you combine them – and repeat them over the course of your working life – the results are likely to set you apart from those who drift through life oblivious to the funding challenge that awaits them in retirement.

Here are some other interesting findings from the report:

- On average, working-age people expect to retire at 64 – three years older than the average retirement age of their parents.

- Almost 15 per cent of people who are not fully retired expect they will never be able to afford to retire from paid employment.

- Entering retirement was accompanied by a fall in income for 79 per cent of retirees. However, this reduction was not matched by a similar drop in spending, with just 54 per cent experiencing a fall in outgoings once they retired.

- 59 per cent of today's retirees say their preparations for retirement turned out to be at least adequate. However, 38 per cent feel they did not prepare adequately. Of those, only 54 per cent realised they were unprepared before retiring.

- Of the retirees who have been unable to achieve all their retirement aspirations, nearly half (46 per cent) cite health reasons, while 45 per cent have less money to live on than they envisaged.

- 34 per cent of 55-64 year-olds have semi-retired, and over half of 25-34 year-olds expect to do so at the same age.

The notion of semi-retirement is well and truly on the rise. In recent years, it has been encouraged by the federal government, with tax incentives for Australians aged 55-plus who have been able to reduce their working hours while accessing their superannuation in the form of a tax-effective income stream (though since July 2017, the appeal of this strategy has reduced following changes to the tax treatment of such income streams). The idea is to encourage more Australians to continue working (and paying tax) in some capacity in their 50s and 60s, rather than ceasing employment altogether. Benefits accrue to the semi-retiree in the form of more workplace flexibility, in addition to continued generation of income and savings, while the nation's finances receive a boost (as more older Australians contribute to the tax base, while delaying the point at which they ultimately draw down on any welfare payments to which they may be entitled).

HSBC's research also explored the motivations of those who choose to transition to semi-retirement. The top 10 reasons are as follows:

1. I would like to keep active/keep my brain alert (52 per cent).

2. I like working and want to continue in some capacity (44 per cent).

3. I would like an easy transition into retirement (38 per cent).

4. I cannot afford to retire full-time (30 per cent).

5. I no longer need to work full-time (22 per cent).

6. I need to bridge a shortfall in my retirement income (19 per cent).

7. I am still paying off my mortgage (16 per cent).

8. I am still paying other debts (12 per cent).

9. Health reasons and physical demands of my work (12 per cent).

10. My household expenditure is higher than I envisaged (9 per cent).

You can learn much from those who have already made their own transition to retirement. Every journey is different, and all retirees have their own motivations and priorities. Below is a summary of insights from HSBC's survey participants, providing an excellent starting point for anyone thinking about life after work.

PRACTICAL STEPS TOWARDS
A BETTER RETIREMENT

ACTION 1: DON'T RUSH RETIREMENT

There is a view among retired people that they may have been too hasty in giving up paid employment. Nearly two-thirds (64 per cent) who entered semi-retirement wished they had stayed in full-time employment longer. This regret is largely for positive reasons, with many retired people seeing work as a crucial way of keeping the body and mind active.

ACTION 2: DON'T RELY ON ONE SOURCE OF RETIREMENT INCOME

Current retirees have, on average, three different sources of retirement income, wisely choosing not to generate all of their income from one place. Spreading their sources of retirement income, and the associated risks, means that not all their eggs are in one basket.

ACTION 3: PLAN YOUR RETIREMENT WITH FAMILY IN MIND

Rather than family ties loosening in future, your family should continue to be a major consideration in retirement planning (and may even grow in importance for the next generation). While many people (40 per cent) aspire to travel extensively during their retirement, nearly half (49 per cent) of current workers expect to have some financial responsibilities towards others, even when they themselves are retired. This includes ongoing financial responsibilities for their adult children, as well as supporting frail, elderly parents.

ACTION 4: BE REALISTIC ABOUT YOUR RETIREMENT OUTGOINGS

Many working people assume their income needs will fall once they enter retirement. Yet 52 per cent of people in retirement have seen no reduction in their outgoings, and 17 per cent have seen their outgoings increase. Although people are familiar with the concept of increasing life expectancy, the consequent increase in medical and nursing care costs may not be well understood, as people are still not doing enough to prepare themselves for these potential costs.

Source: HSBC Future of Retirement: Life After Work

STRATEGY CORNER

'Strategy without tactics is the slowest route to victory.
Tactics without strategy is the noise before defeat.'

SUN TZU

I wrote this book to explore the changing retirement landscape, the economic opportunities of an ageing population, and to draw inspiration from the stories of a generation busily redefining the retirement life stage in pursuit of meaning and purpose.

Over the past decade, I have been fortunate enough to build an award-winning consultancy providing retirement planning advice to families from all walks of life. In writing this book, my aim is not to provide a financial playbook or a detailed 'how-to' of financial-planning strategies. Everyone has unique needs when it comes to planning for their future, and these are best addressed in a personalised strategy that responds specifically to each individual's dreams, objectives, preferences, time horizon and risk tolerance.

But in reflecting on hundreds of retirement planning conversations over many years, there are a few principles and observations that I feel are worth sharing. These are a useful starting point for anyone beginning to think more deeply about planning the next phase of their life.

Observation # 1: Writing down and committing to a carefully considered set of goals, which are meaningful to you and your family, boosts your probability of success.

I am an advocate of working purposefully towards a set of financial and non-financial goals that are meaningful to you and your family. In any field of endeavour, the most effective starting point is sitting down and assessing your current situation, before carefully considering your values, goals and priorities for the future, in order to articulate where you would ultimately like to go. Whether you are planning your financial future or preparing for a half-marathon, the process of goalsetting is just as powerful in maximising your chances of success. Or as American author and consultant Denis Waitley once said, 'The results you achieve will be in direct proportion to the effort you apply.'

Dr Gail Matthews is a clinical psychologist at the Dominican University of California who has conducted research into goalsetting and overcoming barriers to success. In a 2015 study, Gail divided 267 participants into five groups.

- Group one was asked to simply think about business-related goals they hoped to accomplish within a four-week block.

- Group two was asked to write down their goals.

- Group three was asked to write down their goals in addition to making action commitments.

- Group four was asked to write down their goals in addition to making action commitments and sharing their goals with a friend.

- Group five was asked to do all of the above while also sending weekly progress reports to their friend.

The research found that participants were 42 per cent more likely to achieve their goals when they were written down, and 50 per cent more likely to achieve their goals when, in addition to being written down, they were accompanied by action commitments and progress reports.

Observation #2: People who do the work to ensure they generate surplus cash flow each year are far more likely to achieve their financial potential.

This seems obvious, but the core of effective financial planning is doing the work to ensure you spend less than you earn. Once that is the case, you have genuine choices about how you deploy that surplus to build wealth over the long term. You can then engage in conversations about whether your surplus will be directed to additional home loan repayments, extra super contributions, property investments or growing a business. Perhaps some combination of the above makes sense in the context of the goals that matter to you.

In retirement, having insights into the amount you need to generate each year to fund your lifestyle is critical, and your plan should be geared towards ensuring you can achieve this level of income from the financial resources available to you.

Precious few people enjoy the process of 'budgeting', but in this day and age there are countless tools and apps to make the process infinitely less painful. As such, there are no excuses not to have a handle on your incomings and outgoings.

Observation #3: Save early, save often.

This isn't rocket science. Once you have a surplus of income over expenditure in your household, deploying your surplus on a consistent basis is a proven way to build wealth over the long term. I have witnessed countless clients on modest incomes amass retirement savings in excess of $1 million, simply by making use of the contribution limits available to them over an extended period of time. One of the most effective ways you can deploy your surplus cash flow is via salary sacrifice to your super fund. All that means is that you forgo a proportion of your salary, and, rather than receive it and pay tax at a higher marginal tax rate, you put it straight into your super account, where it's only taxed at 15 per cent on the way in. You then receive a concessional rate of tax on fund earnings along the way, and your super is potentially received tax-free when you eventually retire (up to relevant limits).

There are two benefits when you salary sacrifice into your super account. The first is that you save on income tax each year. Cumulatively, that really adds up over the course of a career. The second benefit is that you save more proactively for your future, and allow the power of compounding more time to work its magic. And so not only is your employer putting away 9.5 per cent of your salary, but you're also consciously, regularly and deliberately building your savings pot. When you do arrive at age 60 or later, if you choose to access that money, your future self will thank you.

In July 2017, the government is telling you $25,000 is the annual limit you can add to super as a combination of your compulsory employer contributions and any salary sacrifice contributions you choose to make. The opportunity to reduce your income tax while turbocharging your retirement savings is yours for the taking.

Observation #4: Depending on how much income you need to enjoy a comfortable retirement, you may not need anywhere near $1 million in savings.

The January 2017 changes to the Age Pension eligibility criteria were some of the most significant in history. The estimates are that while 170,000 individuals received a modest increase to their entitlements, some 230,000 Age Pension recipients experienced a reduction, and around 90,000 lost their benefits altogether. These were major changes that sent a strong signal to the community. That is, if the government deems you to be of sufficient financial means, you are increasingly on your own.

Yet within the convoluted eligibility criteria for the Age Pension, a new 'sweet spot' has emerged that may give hope to people who are preparing for retirement with no chance of saving anything close to $1 million or more in super.

While more savings is desirable, and will afford you more lifestyle flexibility as you grow older, consider the retired couple with an unencumbered house, $375,000 in a superannuation pension, and another $25,000 in personal assets. As at July 2017, they are entitled to receive a combined Age Pension of around $33,250 per annum. If they also draw five per cent per annum from their superannuation pension ($18,750 per annum), they are able to generate total combined income of $52,000 per annum tax-free from an investment asset base of just $375,000. Depending on the mix of assets they choose when investing their superannuation pension, it is reasonable to expect that, in most years, they would replace the five per cent of annual pension drawings with fund earnings.

As stated earlier, ASFA estimates that a couple needs $59,971 per year to achieve a comfortable retirement lifestyle, or just $34,855 per year for a modest retirement lifestyle. In the example above, a $52,000 tax-free income in retirement goes a long way towards meeting ASFA's definition of comfortable, and an income of this level is a reasonable expectation for a couple with $375,000 in super.

Remember, 'comfortable' is a subjective term and it will be different for everyone. These standards and benchmarks are useful starting points, but that's all they are. We are all different, we all spend a different amount each year, and we all prioritise different expenditure items in our household budget. Some couples get by on $30,000 per year in retirement, while others need no less than $120,000 per year to meet their needs.

There is no right or wrong. The most important thing you can do here is to conduct an estimate of your actual and expected household expenditure, and then work backwards to ensure you can generate the income you need when you are no longer working. What proportion of your retirement income might come from the Age Pension (if you're eligible)? What amount will you need to draw from your superannuation pension? What other sources of income do you have that can generate passive income in retirement? Is there rental income or dividend income in the picture? Think carefully about the layers of income that will add up to your retirement income target, and aim to hold diversified sources of income so you are not completely dependent on one vehicle for your financial wellbeing.

Observation #5: When contemplating the Australian share market, focus on earnings quality and the long-term value of a growing stream of dividend income.

In the age of the 24/7 media cycle, we are urged daily to focus on very short-term movements in share prices. In every media forum, we are constantly exposed to dramatic and emotive updates about relatively inconsequential changes in the level of the share market. It is not uncommon for online news sites to breathlessly declare there is 'blood on the share market floor' in the wake of relatively minor downward movements in the value of share market indices. Fear sells. We often hear of the many billions 'wiped off the value of shares' when the market opens moderately lower in the morning, but we rarely read about those billions being restored when shares rebound later that day.

In Peter Thornhill's excellent book, *Motivated Money*, he talks about the various types of assets we can all invest in, and he concludes that there are really only two things that grow. One of those is productive enterprise, which you can access by buying shares in companies aiming to grow their profit and dividend. The other is shelter, which is property. Thornhill advocates building a portfolio based on productive enterprise; a quality share portfolio that can deliver you a rising stream of dividend income over time. And in Australia, you're fortunate to be able to do that with the bonus of imputation credits, which add to the tax-effectiveness of your investment income.

Entirely comfortable with the reality that share prices fluctuate, Thornhill prefers to focus on the dividend stream that shares provide over the long term, which he argues is far more predictable and dependable than relying purely on returns from interest-bearing securities. Controversially, he writes, 'I prefer the safety and security of the share market to risky assets like term deposits.'

While acknowledging your capital is safe in term deposits, Thornhill argues that over time, the level of income you generate is not. We have seen this in action from 2008-09 and again in 2017-18, when term deposit interest rates fell from seven to eight per cent per annum to the current level of two to three per cent per annum. If you are solely dependent on term deposits for your income, you have experienced a savage pay cut and your current return after inflation is barely positive.

Investing in shares is not for everyone. Suitability depends on a range of factors, including your risk tolerance, time horizon, investment objectives and long-term goals. However, getting comfortable with the idea of investing in growing companies – as a long-term exercise predominantly designed to generate passive income – is a healthy mindset to adopt.

It is also important to gain an appreciation for the income component of the total return derived from investing in shares. In June 2017, Caitlin Fitzsimmons wrote in *The Sydney Morning Herald* that, between June 2001 and May 2017, 'The ASX 200 delivered a 9.13 per cent annual return or 302.52 per cent in total over that time, but only if you reinvested dividends. The growth based on price change alone was only 3.15 per cent a year.'

So in round figures, while the Australian share market delivered a total annual return of roughly nine per cent between 2001 and 2017, near enough to six per cent per year was made up of dividend income, while share price growth represented just three per cent per year.

The key is to take a long-term approach. Rather than viewing share market investing as a short-term exercise or as a virtual casino where you buy and sell daily, your aim should be to gradually build a portfolio of quality businesses with growing profits and sustainable dividends.

Observation #6: Diversification can reduce risk and increase the consistency of your results.

But of course, it is considered risky to invest in a single asset class to the exclusion of all others. Diversification simply means we spread our investments across a range of different assets that are likely to offer different return characteristics over time. In doing so, we can generally expect to reduce risk and achieve more consistent return outcomes, compared to holding a more limited number of investments.

Over time, the vast majority of the return outcome you achieve is a direct result of this process of 'asset allocation' – or the proportion of your money held in growth assets (such as shares, property, infrastructure and alternative assets) relative to defensive assets (such as bonds, term deposits and cash).

While there is often debate about whether it is preferable to invest in property *or* shares, in my experience, investors tend to do very well over time where they hold a quality combination of *both*.

Observation #7: Be debt smart.

Your relationship with debt, and your understanding of the difference between good and bad debt, will go a long way to determining the financial outcomes you achieve over the long term.

Consolidating debts, making additional and more frequent loan repayments, salary crediting, using offset accounts, and shopping around for the best interest rate at regular intervals, can all help you manage your debt more efficiently.

Used wisely, borrowing to invest can be a powerful long-term wealth-creation strategy, but it is essential to understand the risks and it is important to do your homework to ensure the asset(s) you buy have a reasonable probability of growing in value over time.

Observation #8: Strategy, structure, discipline - ownership decisions matter.

Superannuation is sometimes mistakenly described as a 'bad investment' when, in fact, superannuation is just a tax structure in which you can hold assets tax-effectively and invest for the long term. As far as tax structures go, it is pretty much the best deal in town for retirees. At the time of writing, you can hold up to $1.6 million in a superannuation pension account and pay no tax on the earnings. In fact, most investors even receive a tax refund each year from franking credits, where Australian shares are part of their portfolio.

So putting time and effort into the way you structure your assets, which is really about who owns what, is important. Because, just like progressively saving year in and year out has a powerful compounding effect, if you can progressively reduce tax legitimately, logically and legally each year, the compounding benefit to your financial position really adds up.

Questions you need to answer include: What name should we hold assets in? What should we hold in a superannuation pension environment? What might we hold jointly? What might a family trust hold (if that makes sense for us)? And are there any other structures we should consider to ensure we're paying our fair share of tax, but no more?

Observation #9: Understand the implications of trade-offs.

In isolation, many of the principles in this section serve as useful guidance for the behaviours that will assist you in achieving success over the long term.

But of course, life is never straightforward, and you will often need to make decisions about trade-offs. While generating surplus cash flow each year is an excellent start, you then need to make decisions about where to direct those extra funds. Perhaps additional home loan payments, salary sacrifice contributions or an investment property make sense. It may be that some combination of all three is a worthwhile course of action in your circumstances.

The right decision may depend on many factors – your short and long-term goals, home loan interest rates, your marginal tax rate, expected returns on your investments, your risk tolerance, your personal investment preferences, the property market cycle, and so on.

Understanding the trade-offs, and making good financial decisions, is easiest when you have defined your objectives and you can reconcile various potential scenarios with what it is you are trying to achieve over the long term.

Observation #10: Investors who are able to 'turn down the noise' tend to do well over the long term.

Investment is a long-term exercise, and the biggest challenge you face is that you live in a world that is obsessed with what's happening 'right now'. You're bombarded with hourly updates on stock market movements. Currency movements and interest rate decisions are dramatised, as though our lives depend on these short-term gyrations and market fluctuations. But nothing could be further from the truth.

If you adopt a long-term mindset that acknowledges there will *always* be noise, but consciously recognise and look past the distractions, you'll maximise your chances of success on your financial journey. Remember, successful investing is a marathon – not a sprint.

Bringing it all together

We've covered a lot of ground in this section so, before we move on, allow me to sum up the key points:

- Set goals that are meaningful to you and your family (and write them down).

- Do the work to ensure you generate surplus cash flow each year.

- Deploy your surplus cash flow to a suitable combination of debt reduction and asset accumulation, taking into account your short, medium and long-term goals.

- Understand the retirement planning system and seek to layer your income sources.

- Treat the share market as a long-term activity to generate a growing stream of tax-effective income.

- Diversify your asset base to reduce risk, take control and improve the consistency of your investment outcomes.

- Understand the different types of debt and use leverage to your advantage (where appropriate).

- Understand the implications of trade-offs.

- Think through ownership decisions to ensure you invest as tax-efficiently as you can.

- Turn down the noise and focus on the long term.

- Seek professional advice to help you reach you true potential.

That brings us to the end of Part 4. Now that we've covered the financial considerations of retirement, it's time to consider all of the other aspects.

The following pages feature a collection of stories that highlight the many ways in which the older generation is redefining this phase of life in response to the changing retirement landscape.

This is a generation that is full of life. A generation that is working longer (for reasons of choice or necessity), transitioning to flexible work arrangements, starting businesses, connecting online, travelling in record numbers, getting physically active, participating in fundraising, embracing their creativity, volunteering for a range of causes, and juggling caring responsibilities – often for multiple generations.

An example is worth a thousand theories, and there is much you can learn from the retirement experiences of others. The insights, wisdom and experiences of those who have embarked on their own retirement journey can serve as a useful guide for anyone beginning to visualise and plan their transition to the next phase of life.

PART 5

INSPIRING STORIES AS A GENERATION REDEFINES RETIREMENT

WORKING LONGER: A LIFE OF SERVICE AND CONTRIBUTION

'One person can make a difference and everyone should try.'

JOHN F. KENNEDY

When Professor Ross Homel, AO, 67, explains that 20 per cent of Australian children live in poverty, it makes you stop and think. It is a jarring statistic that doesn't seem to reconcile with the reality that we live in one of the most prosperous nations in the world in a period of unparalleled wealth.

Ross is Foundation Professor of Criminology and Criminal Justice at Griffith University in Brisbane. He has published six books, more than 150 peer-reviewed papers, and won awards for his research on the prevention of crime, violence and injuries, and the promotion of positive development and wellbeing for children in socially disadvantaged communities. In 2008, he was appointed an Officer in the General Division of the Order of Australia (AO) for services to education and criminology, and he was short-listed for 2009 Australian of the Year.

Ross has devoted his academic career to serving the community through his groundbreaking research and community safety initiatives. In 1982, while in his 20s, Ross's research and advocacy led to the introduction of the first mass random breath testing activities in New South Wales.

More recently, Ross has chosen to focus on improving conditions for children growing up in disadvantaged communities.

'We know from oodles of research that the stressors of poverty on parents and children produce all sorts of negative consequences for those individuals and for society. My current philosophy is about early prevention – getting in early to create the conditions that maximise the chances that children can flourish, rather than end up in the justice system, on the streets, or just withdrawn, anxious and depressed, and performing throughout their life at a much lower level than they have a right to expect,' he says.

Ross decided to embark on a life of community contribution as a teenager when he joined the Methodist Church, where the idea of service was reiterated on a regular basis.

Ross doesn't view retirement in a traditional way. His likely retirement transition is more closely aligned to the emerging pattern of the future, which will see Australians remaining engaged in the workforce in flexible ways for longer.

Ross remains passionate about his work at Griffith University, and fully intends to continue in his role until age 70. At that point, rather than cease involvement in research and teaching activities, Ross envisages a transition that will ideally allow him to continue to pursue his passions, but at a less frenetic pace, thus allowing for a greater balance in life.

'I turn 70 in 2019. I'm very strong and fit, and have a lot of energy at the moment, but I do know it is unlikely I will be able to sustain that full level of energy, and I don't actually want to because it is time taken away from my family and my community, and from other projects I am interested in doing. I won't stop working when I turn 70, but I will hopefully move through to an Emeritus Professor role, and I want to continue doing all the good things I enjoy through the university – particularly writing articles and books, and influencing public policy. In many ways, I'll be glad not to have to do all the committees and administration I do now. I'll be glad to give lectures when I want to, not when I'm required to do so,' he says.

Making an ongoing contribution matters to Ross. He feels retirement works best when viewed as a transition, which has the potential to free you up for more meaningful activities. He says, 'I think retirement should be seen as a transition from one way of contributing to another.' Ross has many colleagues at a similar life stage, and he knows older Australians have much to offer, but are not always provided with opportunities to continue to use their knowledge and experience as they age.

'I think our society hasn't yet learned how to value the contributions even very elderly people can make. We've got to be more sophisticated about how we utilise the skills of older people. People in their 70s and even 80s – they've still got an enormous amount to contribute, and I'm aware of people in their 80s doing absolutely amazing things. Not everyone will be able to do that, but for those that can it will be an increasing number, and we ought to be drawing on that. Asian cultures have much more respect for their elders – for good reason. It's obviously been functional for those societies to do that.'

Ross likens the need to better engage older Australians in the workforce to the increasing wealth and productivity we have achieved as a society as, in recent decades, women have become far more involved in the workforce. The beginning of that transition is respect for the unique needs and contribution of older workers, and the recognition that higher participation rates among this group of the population delivers benefits throughout society.

'I think that's one of the next big challenges for our society along with problems like mental health. We're in the dark ages in terms of treatment and old age is a bit in the same category. There's still enormous ageism in our society. The country would benefit from a much more creative approach to this.'

Like most people thinking about how their own retirement may unfold, Ross and his wife Beverley have a number of items they would like to tick off together in the years ahead.

'We want to do more travel. We walk cross-country and do cycling and kayaking, and we want to continue to take active holidays for as long as possible. We'd like to engage more with some of the missionary work and social justice programs of the Christian agencies, and we'd like to have the time and energy to be able to devote [more] support [to] a lot of the really creative work those organisations are doing. I would like to get more books written, and the rest of our ambitions revolve around our family. We want to do what we can to see our children move ahead in their lives.

'Another goal in retirement is to do more as a couple that we weren't able to do in our working lives.'

As our conversation draws to a close, I remark that it doesn't quite sound like Ross will be slowing down anytime soon.

'I don't think I know how to do that. It's a bit of a source of tension in my life. You have got to face the reality of mortality, and also the unpredictability of illness and accident.

'Actually, part of the retirement game and part of getting older is actually being very sensible about your mortality. You don't know when something's going to happen that will stop you. Actually, a friend of mine here has gone back to live in England and he said there's a saying he heard from a Jewish friend: "If you want to make God laugh, tell her your plans!"'

CONNECTING ONLINE: LIFE STARTS AT 60

'The word retirement is getting old.'

REBECCA WILSON

One of the more common misconceptions about the baby boomer generation is that they struggle with technology, and have failed to embrace social media and the rise of online communities. Yet according to the 2017 Sensis Social Media Report, an increasing number of over-65s are flocking to the more popular social networking sites. Meanwhile, research from Pennsylvania State University in the US found that older social media users are motivated by the opportunity to reconnect with old acquaintances, maintain their existing relationships, and keep track of the activities of children and grandchildren.

For older Australians, Rebecca Wilson, CEO and founder of Starts at 60 (www.startsat60.com.au), makes staying connected easier than ever. Established in 2012, Starts at 60 is a rapidly growing online community. In a few short years, the news, blog and information site has become one of the world's largest digital media platforms for over-60s.

After watching her parents retire, Rebecca observed that there were few places online where people aged 60-plus could go to share their stories and interact with others at a similar life stage.

'I started the website having watched my parents go through the age of 60 and transform a lot of things in their lives. They changed the way they worked – they went from working full time to part time – they lost a few of their friends to some tragedies, and they wanted to do the trips of their dreams. And they were really out there looking for the things they had been waiting to do for so many years,' she said in an interview on *Weekend Today*.

'Having watched them, I looked around at the internet and realised that there wasn't anything out there like there was for the mummy market, where you can go and get stories from the people experiencing it. So it seemed logical to create something where they had their own place to go and post, and tell their stories online.

We have established that the passage through the life cycle for over-60s has been evolving at a fast rate. Starts at 60 works because it provides an online community where over-60s can congregate and share the ways in which they are experiencing the life stage in great detail. Turns out the social connectedness that is so important to our wellbeing as we age can also be delivered effectively through an online community.

In my conversations with Rebecca, I am struck by her passion and fierce advocacy for the older generation, and the contribution they make to society. She has a genuine appreciation for their stories, and is at times frustrated at the media's negative portrayal of ageing. Rebecca sees it as her mission to give over-60s a platform where they can share and connect with others in an 'on-demand' way that works for them.

It is June 2017 and we are chatting about the rise in popularity of Starts at 60. This is a business on a steep growth trajectory – Rebecca reports growth of more than 50 per cent in the last few months alone. As we discuss just what it is that makes her online community 'tick', Rebecca describes the way her content simply reflects the priorities and interests of over-60s. The Starts at 60 site provides news and current affairs commentary, while also serving as a platform for online discussion and debate about myriad topics. She has deep insights into the mindset of Australians on the verge of retirement.

'They don't believe they're ordinary and they are in a very strong phase of self-deserve – "This is the time I've been waiting for all my life. The kids have grown up and now it's my turn." The reason the site is successful is because it puts them first. We have an enormous breadth of conversation. Probably the biggest [area] of interest is health and lifestyle. You have 30 per cent of your life to live – what do you want to do with your spare time? You want to be healthy, you want to have things to do that keep you entertained, and you want to go travelling. And then you want to stay up to date. You want to stay with it. I mean, really, that's what our site is.'

The Brisbane-based company is fulfilling a vital need among the baby boomer community via daily opportunities to connect with other members of their generation on issues including health, money, lifestyle, entertainment, property and travel. In fact, in September 2016, such was the demand for more travel-related content from her users, Rebecca established a 'Travel at 60' offshoot, providing exclusive deals from more than 18 major Australian travel brands.

In an October 2013 interview with Ben Hurley of the *Australian Financial Review*, Rebecca summed up the way her target market has completely redefined retirement.

'I think 20 years ago, people were expected to stop work by 60 and sit in a chair all day. This generation of 60 and 70-year-olds is travelling the world, buying cars, buying beach houses and living a different life,' she said.

Since then, participation in the community has risen exponentially. After just four years, the site was attracting 1.5 million unique browsers and five million page views every month. Not surprisingly, this growth trajectory also caught the attention of a number of heavyweight investors interested in a slice of the action.

In September 2016, Seven West Media announced it had secured a 33 per cent shareholding in Starts at 60, in what was described as an investment in one of Australia's fastest growing media brands. The investment allowed the acceleration of the growth of the online community, which has since grown further to achieve 6.7 million page views per month.

At the time of Seven West Media's investment, Rebecca said, 'Our team is proud to be breaking the mould of 60 being old that is so well entrenched in the media industry. Seven's investment brings enormous synergies to support our growth in Australia, and the funding will be used to create the best media and service offerings we can for this generation that has embraced us online.

'It's about the people in the community and their stories. They're on social media at all hours of the day. We're a bit naïve in thinking they're not out there doing all the social media and more, and using it to connect to their world. And that's why we're really helping to build a community. We're just facilitators but it is an incredible amount of fun.'

Perhaps it is this all-important social interaction that is at the heart of the site's popularity. For those who may not be as willing or able to socialise face to face as they grow older, Starts at 60 provides a valuable forum for regular connection and meaningful interaction: an antidote to the loneliness that sadly characterises life for some older Australians. A 2013 national survey conducted by Just Better

Care found that loneliness and social isolation were among the top concerns for older Australians living at home.

In an August 2015 article published by The Conversation (titled 'For older people, beating loneliness isn't just about where and who they live with'), The Open University's Shailey Minocha and Caroline Holland discussed their research, stating, 'Online social interactions can also be a path to greater social inclusion, with a positive effect on wellbeing. Wherever someone is living, when increasing frailty or other life changes start to impact on their quality of life, making sure they are digitally included could be another way to overcome isolation and loneliness.'

In addition to online forums aimed exclusively at over-60s, another trend making waves among older Australians is retirement 'coaching'.

SENIORPRENEURSHIP: RISE OF THE RETIREMENT COACH

'Don't simply retire from something;
have something to retire to.'

HARRY EMERSON FOSDICK

After a 30-year career as a leader and senior executive in the finance and investment industry, Jon Glass was ready for a new chapter, but he wasn't ready to retire. Jon has a PhD in Pure Mathematics from Cambridge University. He was also the Chief Investment Officer of Media Super, among other senior leadership positions in Australia.

Rather than retire to a life of leisure – and after doing some specific training - Jon established a retirement coaching consultancy, 64 Plus (64plus.com.au), to share his experience and insights in order to help others make a more successful transition from the working years to the next stage of their lives. As stated earlier, while there is a tremendous amount of focus on preparing financially for life after work, many simply do not give the same level of attention to the non-financial preparation needed to achieve fulfilment.

The longer you live, the more carefully you need to think about how you spend those extra years to maximise your health and wellbeing, and achieve a meaningful life. The definition of 'meaning' differs for everyone, but the research suggests there are some common activities that improve the probability you will find happiness beyond the working years.

While the social structure of retirement has been with us for the past 100 years or so, retirement coaching is a relatively recent phenomenon. Its relevance has heightened in line with longer life expectancies, which mean more than ever, there are benefits in planning consciously for retirement – not just financially but socially, emotionally, mentally and physically.

Jon points out that the demand for retirement coaching is increasing for two reasons. 'Firstly, executive coaching has been popular in the workplace for some time, but not a long time. Secondly, the baby boomers represent a large cohort of retirees – the largest we have seen in this country,' he says.

So, what sort of conversation can you expect when sitting down with a retirement coach? For those on the threshold of retirement, Jon hears these sorts of expressions:

- I have no idea what I will do, but I will think about it when the time comes.

- I can't leave work yet because there is no one who can do my job if I leave.

- Work stimulates me and provides me with friends.

Among retired people, Jon is more likely to hear these expressions:

- I really need to get out more.

- I suffer RDS (relevance deprivation syndrome). I used to be in demand.

- I am a slave to my free time.

Jon works with his clients to explore some of the major questions that will confront you when you decide to transition to life beyond your career (regardless of what form that may take). What is truly important? How would I like this phase of life to unfold? What are the goals and objectives that matter to me and my family? What is my purpose in life and am I living in alignment with that purpose?

Some of the questions coaches ask are designed to encourage pre-retirees to think deeply about their identity before and after retirement, and, importantly, how they might structure their life in retirement in order to fill the void that is often left when full-time work ceases.

For example, what combination of casual or part-time work may appeal? What hobbies might you pursue? What community activities could you participate in? What are your travel priorities?

'The job of the coach is to listen carefully to these individual expressions to get to the heart of the matter, which, put simply, is to locate that person's meaning in life post-work,' Jon says.

Jon encourages clients to think creatively about the life-changing transition they are embarking on. 'For example, in many cases, a person may never have worked for themselves. Rather, always for other people. So, one definition of retirement is that you become your own boss and employee. Are you going to be a kind boss?'

Jon is, of course, an advocate of retirement coaching services. But before you engage a retirement coach, he says you must first begin a dialogue with yourself and the people who are most important to you.

'I would hope that the mind of a worker in, say, their mid-50s will turn to consider these matters. I think the average person does this with their finances – and that is good. But for their emotions, it seems that our society hasn't yet grasped the nettle. Individuals should commence a dialogue with family members and friends at around this time. Test their reactions. After all, post-work is not an isolated event.'

GLOBETROTTING: THE WORLD IS YOUR OYSTER

'The world is a book and those who do not travel read only one page.'

SAINT AUGUSTINE

The baby boomers have an insatiable appetite for international travel, and there is no doubt they are exploring the world in record numbers. According to the Australian Bureau of Statistics, in the five years to 2016, there was an 80 per cent jump in the number of Australians aged 65-74 taking overseas holidays. Even the over-80s are travelling abroad in record numbers, with a 12 per cent increase over the same period.

The trend is being driven by the availability of affordable airfares, the proliferation of cruise ship holiday options, the rise of online comparison and booking sites, the relative good health of retirees, and an adventurous spirit among older Australians determined to tick a growing number of global destinations off their bucket list.

Scott Hirst is the Managing Director of Pure Traveller – an independent, family-owned travel agency creating unique holiday itineraries for many over-50 clients. Since commencing in 2011, the family business has grown by around 30 per cent per year, due to the increased demand among older Australians for unique travel experiences.

'Predominantly our clients are between 55 and 75, who are either just finding their travelling shoes or who are seasoned travellers who appreciate the experience and insights we offer. Most are multi-country trip planners who make the most of every trip they do. They travel two to three times per year, including one big international trip and a couple of smaller trips to places in Asia, New Zealand and the South Pacific,' he says.

'Most of our over-60 clients prefer customised itineraries. Whether it's sleeping bags in the Serengeti, five-star luxury in Paris, or a great rail journey, we help create the perfect holiday experience. Nothing is out of scope – we have hired the Monza racetrack in Italy for a group of clients, organised a fly fishing expedition to Scotland, and we recently had three generations of a family visit a site of significance in Borneo where a relative was held as a POW during the war.'

I am curious as to the latest countries of choice for Scott's globetrotting clientele, and he indicates there is a shift away from some of the more traditional destinations.

He says 'Canada and Alaska are very popular destinations, as is Europe, but more recently we have had more demand for road-tripping in the United States, and South American trips to places like Patagonia, Argentina, Peru, Galapagos, and even Antarctica. It has never been more cost-effective to visit South America.'

Scott also mentions the rising popularity of cruise holidays, and notes a growing number of grandparents taking their kids and grandkids on a cruise.

'Why not? Unpack once, there is something for everyone to do, you have meals together, and it is all very cost-effective.'

Since retiring in 2012, Tony and Trish Hartley have become prolific overseas travellers. I am more than a touch envious as they enthuse about their upcoming eight-week adventure around Scandinavia and the UK. Having ticked off more than 15 countries in the last five years, I enquire as to whether such frequent overseas holidays had been on the agenda as Tony and Trish approached retirement.

Tony says, 'Well I was still watching the pounds and the pennies at that stage, and I didn't realise that we could do as much as we have done. But we've realised we've got no money worries and we like travelling, so that's what we do ... We're very fortunate.'

Drawing inspiration from online travel offers like Luxury Escapes, holidays advertised in the Sunday newspaper, and their local travel agent, Trish is always on the lookout for the next overseas adventure. 'Every year I like to think we're going to do a decent-sized trip, or we might do two smaller ones.' In most cases, she does her due diligence online before confirming the couple's preferred accommodation options, and Tony is not shy about leaving feedback on their experiences on websites like TripAdvisor.

As we discuss their growing array of passport stamps, the conversation turns to travel highlights and Trish and Tony's more memorable overseas holidays since retiring.

Tony says, 'I was doubting India, but loved every moment of it – it was absolutely brilliant. The chaos on the roads, the friendly people, all the history.'

Trish agrees, 'I loved India, and we went at the end of November, which was a good time because it wasn't as hot and humid. We saw the Taj Mahal, but that was nothing compared to all the other historical sites we visited,' she says.

Japan was another favourite trip of Tony's. 'We went there at the cherry blossom time. It's very fickle – the rain puts it off; the wind puts it off. There must have been a hundred million cherry trees, and they were all in blossom when we were there – it was marvellous. We saw Mount Fuji – right to the top – there was no cloud on Mount Fuji, and that is rare!' he says.

In addition to planning the itinerary of your dream holiday, staying informed of travel warnings has become part and parcel of the international travel experience, and not all destinations are considered to be as safe as they once were.

Five days prior to my interview with Tony and Trish, a suicide bomber killed 22 innocent people at an Ariana Grande concert in Manchester, England. Less than two weeks later, eight people were killed and 48 were injured when terrorists drove a van at pedestrians on London Bridge, before embarking on an horrific stabbing rampage in nearby Borough Market. Such attacks have become more frequent in Western Europe and the United Kingdom.

In the wake of such atrocities, political leaders deliver obligatory words of reassurance, urging people to continue with their travel plans and to carry on with their lives. Any other course of action is portrayed as a victory to those who seek to replace freedom with fear.

And it appears the travellers of the world are heeding this advice. According to the UNWTO World Tourism Barometer, international tourist arrivals increased by 3.9 per cent in 2016 to more than 1.2 billion. In other words, around 46 million more people participated in international travel in 2016 relative to the prior year.

Yet within those numbers, there are identifiable trends that suggest that while people are still willing to travel, they are increasingly wary of parts of the world where terrorist attacks are on the rise, and some choose alternative destinations for their overseas holidays. While France remains the world's most popular tourist destination with around 83 million international visitors every year, a series of major terrorist attacks have had a noticeable impact on the tourism sector. In a February 2017 article in the *Independent*, 'Paris Tourist Numbers Drop Due to Fears Over Further Terror Attacks', Rachel Hosie points out that 'The capital city and the Ile-de-France region which surrounds it, welcomed 1.5 million fewer holidaymakers in 2016 compared to 2015 … This 0.8 per cent drop has cost the area 1.3 billion Euros, which is a 6.1 per cent fall in takings from 2015.'

As Tony and Trish discuss the issue of geopolitical risk and travel plans, they are resolute in their approach. Tony says, 'I take it in my stride. It does worry me a little, but I'm not going to let them win, and I don't want to stay in my backyard. I can do that anytime!'

And the next countries on the bucket list? Trish would like to visit Malta while Tony looks forward to seeing more of Spain and Portugal.

FUNDRAISING: OLDER BUT DEFINITELY NOT INVISIBLE

'We are never really happy until we try to brighten the lives of others.'

HELEN KELLER

The cliché is that when people get older, they fade into the background of society. However, in reality the opposite can be true. Just consider the story of Margaret-Anne Hayes, who has raised more than $200,000 for cancer research, via Can Too, since turning 67. (Can Too is a non-profit program raising funds for cancer research, along with awareness of cancer prevention, via physical challenges such as runs, ocean swims and triathlons.)

In an address to the House of Representatives in June 2015, former Federal Member for Berowra, Philip Ruddock, praised Margaret-Anne's efforts. 'The challenge to every member is to identify a constituent who can do as much as Margaret-Anne in raising money for cancer research. She plans to hit the target of half-a-million dollars, and she is doing this through feats such as holding balls at our Hornsby RSL. She has trained other groups of fundraisers, who, in turn, have raised $1.5 million. She has sold her homemade chutney, she has shaved her head, and she has even skydived from a plane at the age of 73. I have been very fortunate to know her and to support her activities.'

Margaret-Anne, 77 at the time of writing, is a resident of Sydney's upper north shore and has a zest for life that belies her years. She ran her first half-marathon at 68 and, despite being terrified of heights, at age 76 she skydived for the second time to raise more funds for vital cancer research.

I asked what went through her mind as she prepared to jump out of a perfectly functioning plane on the climb to 15,000 feet.

'Sheer terror! I can't tell you what I was saying because it is unprintable. Anyway, this gorgeous young girl sat beside me on the plane and we both held hands. I don't know who was comforting who – I think she was comforting me and so I'm thinking to myself, "It's okay, Margaret-Anne – don't panic, don't panic." And then, of course, it seems like an eternity. All of a sudden you hear this *whoosh* like a tornado, and it all happens incredibly quickly. I remember a gorgeous young man saying, "Feet underneath, boom!" And then out you go. And it is absolute sheer terror! Once you're out, it is very, very cold and it seems a long time before the parachute goes up. And once the parachute goes up, although I was nauseated, I knew I was safe. I said after the first time I would never, ever, ever do it again. This time I mean it!'

Margaret-Anne first caught the fundraising bug in her 50s. As I spoke to her about her story, I asked what motivated her to be such a prolific fundraiser.

'I think the motivating force really was the grief in losing my son, Aaron. He died of a drug overdose in his bedroom on 5 December 2000. And you know the grief is just so paramount and it really never leaves you. I remember contacting beyondblue and other mental health organisations to ask how I could get involved, and help other parents that may be grieving, but I just felt I couldn't cope with anybody else's grief at that point. And so when Can Too started it was such a positive, positive thing. And so my criteria is that whatever I raise is going to stop another mother from losing her son to a physical cancer, whereas I lost my son to a cancer of the soul. His soul gave up,' she says.

Margaret-Anne has had 'ordinary' jobs all her life, and reflects on leaving school at 16. She remembers her father saying, 'Girls just get married and don't have any education.' Margaret-Anne feels like losing her son in such tragic circumstances prompted her to rethink her purpose in life. She feels she came into her own for the first time in her 60s and 70s.

'I've found I've always been interested in people. People have always fascinated me. I love seeing wedding photos, baby photos, dog photos. I love hearing people's backgrounds, especially older folks. Especially now at 77, I've found that I've come into my own. You know I'm an excellent public speaker – I seem to be a bit of a motivator – and suddenly you have people saying, "You are inspirational," and it's actually quite humbling,' she says.

'I think that if you went out a mile from where you are, or a mile from where I am, we would find people that have done equally as much or more than me. You know, ladies that have been the Pink Ladies at the hospital ... They're 85 and they've been doing it for 60 years, and I just think that in society there are so many unsung heroes. People that we just never hear about. We hear about all these stupid pop stars and all these criminals, and I think if we explored society there would be stories like mine – people that are doing wonderful things.

'I'm hoping other people might think if I can manage to run a half-marathon at 68, well perhaps they can stop what they're doing and go to art school. Or perhaps they can change their job and do what they've always wanted to. Or perhaps they can do that swim or something like that. If they go out and perhaps do some fundraising, then that is a win-win situation ... People think that once you're over

50, you don't have a brain in your head, whereas I'm surrounded with brilliant older women.'

Margaret-Anne has a history of rallying others to raise funds for charities that are close to their hearts. I asked her how others can get started with fundraising efforts. She emphasised the importance of participating in fundraising that is an extension of your hobbies and interests.

'What I try and say to people is, "Use your talents." This is what I tell the youngsters when they're trying to raise the money. If you love cooking, then bake muffins and have a bake sale. Have people round and do a dinner and dessert. If you like golf, get involved in the committee of the golf club. Now, if people have always been interested in sport ... you might be able to join your local athletics or Little Athletics [club] as a coach or as a citizen's coach.'

Her other piece of advice is to start off small and to focus on what you love doing.

'If you love painting ... start doing some little paintings and sell them and donate the money,' she says.

'If you love quizzes, get together a group of friends ... [and raise money by hosting a] trivia night. Or organise a film night. If you've got half-a-dozen of you, you say, "Right, we're going to [see a] film or have a meal beforehand and we'll all put in an extra $20."'

Margaret-Anne makes the point that every donation counts – and no donation is too small – because you never know quite how close scientists and researchers are to achieving transformational breakthroughs that could potentially benefit countless people.

'The lowest donation I've ever had when fundraising was from an older lady and she gave me three dollars. Now, anybody might think,

"Three dollars? Not even the price of a cup of coffee." But I think if you're on a pension and you give somebody three dollars, that is equal to kings giving millions because she's given it from the heart. That humbles you, and you think, "How unbelievably fantastic." And then I say to people, "It's like a rolling ball. That might be the last three dollars that somebody needs to achieve their goal in Can Too of raising $1,200. That money might then be the last $1,200 needed to make the $100,000 target for a researcher, and then that researcher uses those funds to make a breakthrough that could lead to a drug that helps millions."

'My motto is "Older but definitely not invisible", and so I'm always wearing bright colours or beads or whatever. And you know, one lady said to me the other day – she was right at the top of the hill and she said to me, "I could see this colourful person down there and I knew it would be you, Margaret-Anne." And I think, you know, if I see older women, I always say, "Gee, you look lovely today," or "Gee, that's a lovely blouse," or "Have you just had your hair done?", because older women in particular are invisible.'

VOLUNTEERING: COMBINING HOBBIES AND A DESIRE TO GIVE BACK

'You can live to be a hundred if you give up all the things that make you want to live to be a hundred.'

WOODY ALLEN

Volunteering for causes you are passionate about is an opportunity to make a difference, keep your mind active, and remain involved in the community as you age. Ben, 73, is a proud volunteer who believes firmly in the power of hobbies to achieve greater wellbeing in retirement.

Ben built a career on hard work and company loyalty, which started in the military and ended with back-to-back 20-year stints driving long-haul trucks for Mayne Nickless and Boral. After starting work as a railway clerk at age 14 to help his parents make ends meet, Ben came to the conclusion that a life of adventure was more to his liking. At 19, he joined the army for a six-year stint that straddled the Vietnam War. He still regards that period as the best years of his life.

'They fed me, clothed me and boarded me every day for six years, and I went somewhere different and did something different almost every single day. I thought that was absolutely fabulous,' he says.

While in the army, Ben would meet and marry his wife. But after six years of long absences while on active service, he made the decision to settle his family and bought a house in Sydney's western suburbs. At the age of 25 – with two young daughters, one broken-down car and not very much money – he made the decision to trade a life of adventure for life in the suburbs. Ben rolled up his sleeves and set out to achieve what became known as the Great Australian Dream.

'I did two jobs for eight years, without one single day off. After eight years, I had completely paid for my own house on a good block of land and owned two decent motor cars. I was working an awful lot of hours. I even worked Christmas Day. I had a permanent full-time job driving interstate transport for Mayne Nickless and I did taxi driving as a second job,' he says.

Ben was motivated to work such a demanding schedule to ensure he could provide for his young family and afford them the opportunities he felt mattered.

'I wanted to see my family settled and my children educated, and not worry about having to up stumps every year or two, like I would have had to do if I'd stayed in the army. I was determined to secure my family's future in their own house,' he says.

During the 1990s, while driving long-haul trucks for Boral, Ben had an overwhelming feeling that he had been working too hard for too long, and that something needed to change. In his 50s by this stage, Ben made a conscious decision to set aside some money for retirement, and put some into a series of shorter term 'nest eggs', which would allow him to enjoy the fruits of his labour right now.

'The idea was that I didn't want to squander the good income I had, but I also felt there may not be much left of me in retirement, so I didn't want to save too much either. I wanted to enjoy some of it now in case I didn't last too long,' he says.

As I learn more about Ben's life story, he strikes me as someone who harbours no regrets. But as he reflects on his time in the army, he laments the one mission he would have dearly loved to have been involved in. Ben was a member of the 42nd Transport (Amphibious) Platoon, an exclusive ship-to-shore transportation platoon, and the only amphibious unit in the army at the time.

One of the more intriguing missions of this specialist platoon saw a select twelve members make the voyage to Antarctica each year to resupply the Davis, Casey and Mawson stations. They would sail from Hobart on Boxing Day and would be away for three months. With his adventurous spirit, Ben would have joined the trip in a heartbeat – had he met the prerequisites – but nature conspired against him and it wasn't to be.

'I've always been a skinny little bloke and they only took big, burly fellows – it was a requirement. I wanted to do it but they wouldn't let me because I simply was not big enough to do all the heavy lifting and work involved,' he says.

Many years later, and long after his departure from the army, a 57-year-old Ben read about a company in Christchurch offering two trips a year for tourists wanting to explore the Antarctic bases. As he had started to wind back his hours at work, he decided to take the plunge and tick Antarctica off his bucket list.

'I realised I had the money, I had the time, and I had the opportunity. I thought, "I'm going to do this." It cost me $16,000 for the fare, for 28 days on a very small ship on the worst ocean in the world. There were 48 tourists from 16 different countries on the ship and it was an absolutely mind-blowing experience,' he says.

It was 2008 when Ben's 20-year stint driving for Boral drew to a close. He was tired and ready to slow down, and thus make the transition to the next chapter of his life. He had no shortage of offers for casual and contract driving work, and the flexibility this offered suited him down to the ground.

'I never stop getting offers of work, and that's purely due to my grand résumé of life experiences in transport,' he says.

'There's a limit to how much you can push and I've always been one of those people who has pushed the envelope a bit. So adventure has always been a big thing. It's only in the last three years that I've come to a complete stop and had enough.'

While he has been semiretired since 2008, I ask Ben why he has made a more conscious effort to slow the pace of life in the last three years. He relays a story of his last overseas trip to Europe, where the long-haul flight – and the 'agony of packing and unpacking and carting bags' – made him reluctant to do any more major overseas travel.

'I decided I've been doing it most of my life, and my body is now – for want of better words – simply worn out. When it comes to physical activity, I've worn it out. I've used it to the maximum all my life, and I've been very lucky. I've enjoyed very good health, and I think all physical work has probably helped to retain good health. But now I think I've simply worn everything out. But I don't let it stop me. I think any mental and physical activity helps to subvert the aches and pains you feel. It's a mental discipline,' he says.

When it comes to finding meaningful and fulfilling activities in retirement, Ben is not short on opinions.

'I think your health is a big factor, and I think if you're going to sit home and worry too much about whether you'll last or not, I think that's probably rather negative. I've always been a rather positive person,' he says.

In retirement, Ben channels this positivity into volunteering and a desire to give back to the community. Among many activities, he has spent time teaching young indigenous men to drive and to obtain a motor vehicle licence, in order to build their sense of achievement and self-worth.

He says 'The greatest satisfaction of all comes from doing things for people who have nothing. These young men come from alcohol and drug-addicted parents, and they have never had anybody treat them with civility, and instil discipline in their lives.' he says.

Hobbies also play a key role in Ben's pursuit of purpose, and he is a firm believer in the importance of maintaining hobbies in retirement. Since securing his first job as a clerk at Sydney Trains as a 14-year-old, he has held a keen interest in railway history. Today he spends three days a week volunteering at the Australian Railway Historical Society in Redfern, scanning and indexing historical images and documents, which capture the evolution of Sydney's rail network and associated stories dating back to the mid-1800s. As he describes his passion for railway history, you get the sense it is almost a meditative pursuit.

'Hobbies or interests are essential for any working person at all. It's important. Even when I was working seven days a week, I would still sometimes spend half an hour reading a magazine about trains. No matter how busy I got, I would have half an hour dedicated to isolated little moments to myself, where everything was wiped from my mind and I just concentrated on my interest,' he says.

'That is the strongest recommendation I would put to anybody. As you have probably discovered, many people are at loose ends when they retire. They do not have a personal interest that is all theirs. Some people want to build a yacht in their backyard. Some people want to paint a picket fence or grow flowers, and some people want to play golf or go fishing, which is another way to see your mates.'

As Ben says, there is no shortage of hobbies you can take up.

GETTING ACTIVE: OVERCOMING ADVERSITY AND TAKING ON NEW CHALLENGES

'Grow old along with me!
The best is yet to be.'

ROBERT BROWNING

In October 2012, Jenny Kennedy (aged 65 at the time) remembers waking up one Thursday morning with a bloated stomach and some pain in her lower left side. She thought little of it, but decided that if it hadn't improved the following day, she would see her GP, Dr Catherine Li.

By Friday, Jenny's discomfort was growing, so she went along to see Dr Li who was surprised to find Jenny's entire abdomen was 'hard'. Initially suspecting a bowel obstruction, Dr Li consulted a colleague who advised a CT scan. The scan was organised for the same afternoon and Jenny was told to come straight back to the clinic. The scan showed a 'major cystic lesion' in the form of a sizeable ovarian cyst, so Dr Li ordered an ultrasound the following Monday and referred Jenny to a gynaecological oncologist. To make a harrowing situation worse, Jenny had to wait a full week before any oncologists were available as they were all overseas attending a conference.

'That was one of the longest weeks of my life,' Jenny says. 'As the (possibly) cancerous cyst was so big, the fears were that it would have already spread to my other organs, and my doctor was concerned about my lungs as I had a cough at the time. I remember so well the wave of fear that swept through my body when my doctor looked at the ultrasound results and couldn't conceal the alarm in her voice. She said, "We have to prepare for the worst," and I thought she meant I was going to die. But she meant that it could be ovarian cancer.'

Jenny left the doctor's clinic in a daze. Her biggest worry was telling her children, but she rationalised that even if she did have cancer, she wasn't going to die tomorrow. She would still have time. In the days that followed, Jenny describes living in an alternate reality.

'I felt like an alien. Everyone was going about their business – friends were having coffee and laughing, but I no longer felt I belonged to that world. One day I watched a very old lady, stooped over, as she pushed her shopping trolley up the street. I envied her all the years she had experienced that I may not get.'

Jenny eventually met with the surgeon and was told that, until they opened her up, they wouldn't know the extent of the tumour. She had the operation that week and waited for the results to come back from the lab. Another week later, after an agonising wait, Jenny finally had a diagnosis.

'It was with utter amazement that I learned I had a 3.5 kilogram, basketball-sized ovarian tumour removed. The tumour consisted mainly of precancerous cells with a fist-sized cluster of cancerous tissue in the middle. The cancer had not spread and so I was diagnosed with stage 1a mucinous ovarian cancer – this is the only curable stage.'

According to the Australian Institute of Health and Welfare, it is estimated that more than 1,500 new cases of ovarian cancer will be diagnosed each year. There are no early detection tests, and the symptoms are common (abdominal bloating, difficulty eating or feeling full quickly, frequent or urgent urination, back, abdominal or pelvic pain, menstrual irregularities, fatigue, indigestion), so the cancer is more commonly discovered at a later stage, which leads to a poor prognosis. Cancer Council Australia points out that, in 2014, the overall five-year survival rate for women diagnosed with ovarian cancer was just 44 per cent.

Curious, I ask Jenny about any symptoms and warning signs that may have been clues to the mass that had taken up residence in her body.

'One of my initial responses to having a 3.5 kilo tumour growing inside me was to feel utterly stupid – how could I not have known?! I have since found that it is called the silent cancer as the symptoms are so vague and can be attributed to so many other causes. That was the case with me. I did notice over about three months I was developing a bit of a tummy, but I thought that was the result of my age, 64, and my lack of regular exercise. I was a little tired, and people told me afterwards that I was not a good colour – I was looking grey.'

Jenny later discovered that this rarer type of cancer grows to be very large, but spreads slowly. After recovering from surgery, Jenny commenced four months of chemotherapy treatment on the advice of her medical team. While the cancer had been caught relatively early, it was unknown how long the tumour had been growing, and her oncologist felt there was sufficient potential for metastases (the development of secondary cancerous growths) to warrant chemotherapy.

Of her treatment, Jenny says, 'The main side effects were lethargy, depression, loss of appetite and significant weight loss. I recovered from all those but have been left with peripheral neuropathy in my feet. It's not painful but means I have to buy expensive shoes with good support. This I can handle!'

Significant life events and serious health scares often serve as a trigger to question our priorities. This reassessment can lead to profound life changes and personal growth, and this was certainly true for Jenny.

'Having cancer was dreadful, but the silver lining was that I was challenged in so many ways. I have changed profoundly as a result and for that I am grateful. When confronted with possibly dying, I was forced to re-examine my life and my way of thinking – the essence of who I was. The person that I have found is so much happier. She is truer to herself and doesn't worry so much about what people think of her. She is exploring life and doing the things she wants to. She is enjoying making new beginnings, following her passions, and finding ways to be a contributing citizen and a role model for her grandchildren.'

After finishing treatment, Jenny completely transformed her existence. Between ages 65 and 70, she embarked on more new adventures than at any previous time in her life. She:

- Became more open to meeting new friends, and joined a local meet-up group for regular walks and coffee (www.meetup.com).
- Completed a 60-kilometre walk as part of the Weekend to End Women's Cancers.
- Joined a Quest for Life fundraising tour of Bhutan (hosted by Petrea King), which involved trekking in the Himalayas, yoga, sharing stories, and encouraging each other to achieve their dreams (www.questforlife.com.au).
- Participated in a subsequent Quest for Life trip to Italy, Croatia and Slovenia.
- At age 70, signed up with Can Too to train and run a 14-kilometre relay leg of the SMH (*Sydney Morning Herald*) Half Marathon (www.cantoo.org.au).

- Organised a 1960s trivia night and collectively raised more than $8,000 for cancer research.

- Commenced participating in regular five-kilometre park runs (www.parkrun.com.au).

- Signed up to run the City2Surf and the Blackmores Half Marathon.

Jenny's cancer scare gave her a new lease on life, and she credits Petrea King and the Quest for Life Foundation for providing her with the support and inspiration to consciously redesign her life and seek out new beginnings. She recalls a particularly powerful exercise she undertook while trekking in Bhutan in 2014.

'We climbed to Tiger's Nest Monastery where we received a blessing from the Buddhist monk, and we consciously left behind on the mountaintop something in our lives that was holding us back from believing in ourselves. I guess I have spent time examining the ideas, ideals and values that I want to be central to my new life. Quest for Life is a wonderful organisation that supports those goals and helps you arrive [at them],' she says.

A keen distance runner myself, I am intrigued to learn of Jenny's motivations for taking up running for the first time at age 70. Countless studies confirm the importance of remaining active as we age in order to maintain optimal physical and mental wellbeing, and to lower the risk of premature death due to cardiovascular disease and a range of common cancers. According to a 2015 Department of Health report, titled 'Australia's Physical Activity and Sedentary Behaviour Guidelines', people over 65 should participate in 'at least 30 minutes of moderate intensity physical activity on most days'. However, various studies suggest that only around 40 per cent of older Australians exercise to this extent.

Having turned 70, Jenny wanted to do something challenging and memorable, which would also provide a way to improve her fitness. She signed up with Can Too (the same fundraising organisation favoured by fellow retiree Margaret-Anne Hayes), which provides professionally coached group-training programs for its fundraisers. Having never participated in distance running before, the prospect of running 14 kilometres at age 70 was daunting.

'I had never run, except to play chasing games with grandchildren, and I'm certainly not the sporting type. After my first warm-up run of less than a kilometre, I thought I was going to throw up and wondered had I been insane to sign up for something I obviously couldn't do! But the Can Too coach was so skilled and professional, and the group were so encouraging, that I kept going and soon realised that achieving this goal was a definite possibility.'

After 12 weeks of gruelling training, Jenny indeed ran the 14-kilometre relay leg of the SMH Half Marathon in a little over two hours. Feeling a mixture of elation and relief, she crossed the finish line in Sydney's Hyde Park hand-in-hand with two of her grandsons (Oliver and Henry), who had jumped the fence and joined in for the last 100 metres of the event.

Jenny retired from her career as an English teacher and Deputy Principal of an independent school while in her late 50s – a decision driven by the need to devote more time to caring for her mother. Family commitments meant she was unable to retire on her terms, and it would be some years until her health challenges would see Jenny develop new perspectives on her purpose in retirement.

'I now know that retirement is not about preparing for the end. It is about making new beginnings, setting ourselves challenges, and accomplishing amazing goals – just as we have done all our lives!

But now, it's not so much about work or even family – it's more personal. We are at a stage in life where we can contribute so richly to our family, community and beyond. We need to be fit and healthy to do this well.'

I ask what's next, and whether her new-found interest in distance running is likely to continue.

'I'm planning to run in the City2Surf and then complete the Blackmores Half Marathon as my big goal for the year,' she says. 'After that, who knows? Maybe a marathon, if the body permits!'

CREATIVE PURSUITS: EMBRACING A PASSION FOR ART

'The purpose of art is washing the dust of daily life off our souls.'

PABLO PICASSO

Artist Bruce Chanter's father was an accountant with a passion for numbers and helping people. So much so that he was still processing tax returns for a small number of clients at age 90 – just two weeks before he passed away. Bruce chose a different retirement pathway from his father, finishing up in his role as a Senior Manager for a major national retailer at 55, and relocating from Sydney's northern beaches to the picturesque surrounds of Berry, on the New South Wales south coast.

The relocation was driven by Bruce's desire to get away from the pressures of business in order to focus on his passion for art. Prior to his career in the retail industry, Bruce worked in advertising and attended a number of prestigious Sydney art schools. As he reflects on this earlier stage of his life, and associating with subsequent Archibald Prize winner, John Olsen, we conclude that Bruce's time as an artist in the 60s might best be described as his 'creative period'. Many years later, he felt he now had the opportunity to indulge his creative side and revisit his love of painting.

'Here was the dream – retire right on 55 and change my career. I wasn't thinking of it as putting my feet up and reading a newspaper.

I had an intense interest and desire to become a more skilled artist – a craftsman – and the idea of becoming a master painter appealed to me. So it was a matter of changing my occupation, but to one which I was not necessarily financially tied to. So [I had] the idea of coming to the coast and setting up a studio because I have the artistic ability – I never lost that.'

Bruce and his wife Patricia built their new home at Berry and included a purpose-built artist's studio. After spending the first couple of years studying art books, and attending classes run by a local artist, Bruce began painting and exhibiting. He decided to combine a love of travel with his art and, during holidays to Italy and France, Bruce would take photos of picturesque villages, cafés and scenic landscapes as inspiration for his paintings, which would later feature in his exhibitions.

'I was always looking for the real world, and the old villages ... the back canals of Venice where, you know, real-world people obviously live. I'm looking through the camera and visualising a painting. I got a lot of material from that and we brought it back, and I did a series of paintings on Paris and Venice, and themed my exhibitions around those subjects.'

Bruce has gone on to hold exhibitions of still life paintings, seascapes and marine works, and he is currently painting a series of pieces for an abstract exhibition. I ask him what it feels like to painstakingly produce a series of paintings for exhibition and then to be judged on that work.

'It's really rewarding. I've had a lot of exhibitions, I've been there, and I've had tremendous feedback. I think selling art is like selling houses. You've got to find just the right buyer who loves it,' he says.

Bruce's retirement transition was well planned and methodically timed, so I am not surprised he has some well-formed views on the prerequisites for a fulfilling retirement.

'I think primarily you need to be occupied and do something you enjoy doing,' he says. 'It's a major stage of your life. Your life is your work for a long period of time and I think a lot of people fall into a vacuum when they retire and say, "What am I going to do with myself?" Maybe I was lucky because I had some talent in an area that was not related to my work, but I think everybody's got something. And if you can find something that really interests you ... it might be studying law, it might be making wooden tables, it might be painting, or something with your hands. Everybody's different, but I think a crucial element is to have something that interests you, that can occupy you, and give you some satisfaction. And I think you've got to have something to look forward to.'

Indeed, in much of the commentary we read about the inputs to happiness as we age, 'having something to look forward to' is commonly quoted. Bruce lights up as he articulates the activity that puts a spring in his step each day.

He says, 'You know, I'm halfway through a painting ... I can't wait to get up tomorrow morning and get back on it, get in front of that easel and start slapping some paint around. You know, it's really great. That's what makes you tick.'

THE CARING CONUNDRUM: HATS OFF TO THE SANDWICH GENERATION

*'Life's most persistent and urgent question is,
"What are you doing for others?"'*

MARTIN LUTHER KING, JR

No two retirement journeys are the same. People decide to transition from their job or business, over an array of time frames, for many different reasons. For some, their body tells them it has had enough and it is time to down tools. Others may be made redundant in their 60s and, in a tough job market, they have very little say in the timing of what turns out to be their involuntary retirement. The ideal is, of course, a carefully planned transition that is conducted on your own terms, but for many reasons this is not always possible. As Scottish poet Robert Burns said, 'The best laid plans of mice and men often go awry.'

For John and Sandra (aged 67 and 66 respectively), their decision to retire meant closing the doors to their family clothing business after some 65 years in operation. Based in Lidcombe in Sydney's western suburbs, their menswear store was established in 1949 (the year John was born) by John's parents, after both returned from serving in World War Two. John's father spent time as a medical orderly in the army in Bougainville in Papua New Guinea, while his mother worked in the Women's Auxiliary Air Force (WAAF) as an electrical fitter.

John says, 'They had quite a different experience in terms of their World War involvement. Mum was posted in Darwin at one stage and spent time stripping down American engines that had been thrown out of the US planes. The Americans used to just throw everything out – all their control panels and stuff – and the Aussie girls used to scavenge the instruments out of them to try and fix the Australian planes up.'

Once John's parents returned from the war, they married and settled down to start the clothing business. John's father was an accountant by trade, while his mother had experience in designing and making clothes, so their respective skills were a useful combination that would see the clothing business trade successfully for decades, supporting multiple generations of the family.

After starting his career as a school teacher, John would join the family business in 1974. He and Sandra would work together with John's father, while Sandra would also juggle looking after the children through the day.

In an era where the Australian Bureau of Statistics tells us that more than 60 per cent of new businesses fail within the first three years, it is a remarkable achievement when a family business can prosper for more than six decades – particularly in the retail industry, where competition and technology have fundamentally changed the game.

It was that changing competitive landscape, and the looming challenges for independent Australian retailers, which led to John and Sandra's decision to cease business and retire in 2014. They were 64 and 63 at the time.

John says, 'The changing marketplace and supplier base started to influence our attitude as to whether we felt it was worth sticking it out much longer, and we ended up deciding it was more worthwhile to sell the property, so I took retirement a year and a bit earlier. But I mean, 65 years in the one spot – we have a lot to be thankful for in that it provided a living for us in that period of time.'

Sandra was also a catalyst for the decision to retire, as she could see the writing on the wall for retailers. She said to John, 'Is this really the way to go, or is it about time we had more time with our kids and we can support them a bit more as well?'

John and Sandra sold the premises that housed the family business, and were pleased with the way they ultimately transitioned to their version of retirement.

Yet their retirement plans did not include overseas travel, playing golf, or planning their next cruise – though I suspect John would like to make a little more use of the 12-foot boat he has parked in his garage! The church plays an important role in their lives, and, selflessly, they view this phase of life as an opportunity to support their children and grandchildren, while Sandra also has significant caring responsibilities for her elderly mother, Dorothy.

One of John and Sandra's sons is the pastor of a Presbyterian Church in Brisbane. Jeff and his wife Naree have two children with special needs – Gemma, 10, and Evan, two. Both were born with Joubert syndrome, a rare genetic disorder that causes abnormal brain development, which can lead to reduced muscle tone, challenges with coordination, and intellectual disability. John describes the condition as 'a breakdown in communication between the brain and the body'.

Gemma and Evan are both legally blind, and neither of them are able to speak.

John and Sandra's commitment to their family is obvious. They roll up their sleeves to assist their Sydney-based sons with everything from housing renovations to childminding and landscape gardening, and they are comfortable travelling to Brisbane on a regular basis to spend time looking after Gemma and Evan, if it allows Jeff and Naree the opportunity for an occasional getaway to refresh and recharge.

'Life's pretty full for them. Jeff, as a minister, has a church with people with needs that he cares for. Only people who observe what it is like for genuine ministers – who want to help people and care for them through all that they're going through – can realise what a burden pastors sometimes carry as they look after a church congregation. His church is now around 75 people, and it was only 38 when he took over five years ago,' says John.

This increasing trend – of individuals spending more time caring for both younger and older generations within their families – has been labelled the rise of the 'sandwich generation'. While the term can be applied to those in their 40s and 50s, it is increasingly common for retirees to shoulder the dual responsibility of supporting their adult children in a variety of ways (financial and non-financial), while also taking on time-consuming caring duties for their elderly parents. John and Sandra take this reality in their stride.

'I don't know how other people think about it, but we see other friends who, at our age, are seeking to support their kids – giving their time to give parents a bit of a break from what's a fairly full routine with family. We're Christians, members of a church, and we have a very active Bible study group, and we're noticing that quite a few of them are busy supporting their kids and grandkids. And where there's a need, even helping them financially, like deposits on houses. We realise that kids today are faced with houses that are a lot more expensive in dollar terms than ours were.'

Just as John and Sandra consciously prioritise time spent supporting their children and grandchildren, Sandra's 89-year-old mother,

Dorothy, still lives at home and also requires a lot of help on an ongoing basis. Sandra takes her to appointments at the doctor, podiatrist and hearing aid clinic, and they are mindful that any time they may spend away from Sydney means a diminished support structure for Dorothy.

John says, 'She doesn't want to leave her home and we look at her and think she'd be a lot better off, even just relationally, to be in a retirement village somewhere where she had more people her own age. She's 89 going on 90, and she's still well enough to go on bus trips and things, but she just could do with having a little bit more interaction with others on a regular basis through the day. I think it'd be good for her.'

I ask John what he feels are the keys to retiring well.

He says, 'My reaction is that what we're doing is quite fulfilling and meaningful. Because it's very personal when you are able to give time to support your own kids. We look at the level of marriage breakdown today, [and] we look at the stress and strain we hear about in the media all the time – about just what working mothers express is the stress for them, and their partners [feel] the same way. And we look at some of the things that are happening in terms of family life ... people are so busy and involved, and we think that kids, as a result, and the future generations, are missing out on a lot of quality family time. So, in our point of view, in any way we can contribute to improving that in our own kids' lives and grandkids' lives, that's important.'

PART 6

RETHINKING RETIREMENT IN PURSUIT OF MEANING, PURPOSE AND ENGAGEMENT

PROTIREMENT: AGEING POSITIVELY ON PURPOSE

'To me, fair friend, you never can be old,
For as you were when first your eye I eyed,
Such seems your beauty still.'

WILLIAM SHAKESPEARE

Earlier, we discussed the financial challenges of retirement. In essence, we are living longer with less workplace certainty and less generous government support, so we need to carefully consider how we plan our finances to support us through those extra years. Many people are choosing to work longer to boost their savings to achieve this.

However, your financial wellbeing shouldn't be your only consideration. Any planning for a rewarding retirement should also consider meaning and purpose. Remember that this is going to be a multi-decade period of your life.

Author of *Live Happier, Live Longer: Your guide to positive ageing and making the most of life,* Dr Tim Sharp, is an expert on positive ageing. In addition to his work as an Adjunct Professor at the UTS Business School and RMIT School of Health Sciences, he is a psychologist, speaker, consultant, writer, coach, and CEO of The Happiness Institute. He holds three degrees in psychology (including a PhD), and runs one of Sydney's oldest and most respected clinical psychology practices.

I was thrilled he was available to share his insights into what makes for a happy and fulfilling experience as you age.

Sharp is a believer in the idea that happiness *can* increase with age, provided you understand some of the proven inputs to your health and wellbeing, and provided you are willing to put effort into the right places. So, where should you focus?

'Firstly, in planning – determining and defining exactly what a "happy retirement" would look like for you – and then clarifying exactly what you need to do to make that a reality in your life,' he says.

While acknowledging that everyone is unique, Sharp goes on to list the most common inputs to a happier and more fulfilling experience in the years following traditional employment:

1. Ensure there is meaning and purpose in your life outside of work.

2. Be physically fit and healthy.

3. Think optimistically about the future and the ageing process.

4. Develop and foster good quality relationships and connectedness within key communities.

5. Have fun!

If these things are missing, older Australians may experience depression, says Sharp.

'As well as all the usual causes of and contributors to depression, there are also some especially concerning ones for older people, none more worrying than isolation and loneliness. Just as good quality relationships are vital for our health and happiness, a lack of these is increasingly being viewed as one of the major health issues for our future with an ageing population. The good news is that as individuals, families and communities, we can recognise this and work together to do something about it,' he says.

As part of the research effort for this book, I sought a range of views by speaking to retirement coaches, workplace experts, academics, business owners, athletes, psychologists, actuaries and finance experts. One of the recurring themes during these interactions was a growing urgency to fundamentally reinvent retirement with a definition that better serves you, as an existing or soon-to-be-retiree, and society more broadly.

Over the years, Sharp has given this topic plenty of thought. In many ways, he was ahead of his time when, in 2014, he proposed a framework referred to as 'protirement'. In his book, he provides a positive vision for how the chronology of retirement might better play out to be a more satisfying and fulfilling transition.

'In protirement, people plan for and conceptualise a positive transition, gradually, from full-time work to a "portfolio" of employment, voluntary, social and recreational activities. I've no doubt this approach will become increasingly popular and, in fact, the norm,' he says.

Sharp says that while it's important to prepare financially for retirement (or protirement), you must also prepare mentally and emotionally for growing older.

'I don't think most prepare very effectively in these areas at all. Since compulsory superannuation was introduced in Australia in the early 1990s, most people have essentially been forced to plan and prepare financially for retirement. Even if many don't do this as well as some would like, almost everyone is doing at least something in the financial domain ... You can have all the money you like. Yet if you're sick and tired and unhappy and lonely, then no amount of dollars in the bank will make for a happy retirement.'

So, how can you ensure a happy, fulfilling retirement? By ensuring you have something to retire *to*, rather than something to retire *from*.

WE ALL NEED SOMETHING TO RETIRE TO

'The purpose of life is a life of purpose'

ROBERT BYRNE

It is often said you need something to retire to, not just something to retire from. One of the best examples of this in modern society is in the sporting arena, where occasionally we hear of highly successful athletes who struggle to make the transition to life after sport. There is much you can learn from the challenges some elite athletes face when confronted with the prospect of retirement from their chosen career. Many achieve extraordinary feats in their chosen field, only to retire at a relatively young age to find a gaping void in their lives that is painfully difficult to fill.

In April 2017, the ABC's *Four Corners* program profiled a number of sportsmen and women, and explored the challenges they faced in adapting to their new reality when the siren sounded on their careers.

Former Wallaby Brendan Cannon played for his country on 42 occasions between 2001 and 2006, before retiring in 2007 (age 34) due to a serious neck injury. Cannon highlights the difficulty associated with giving up a career you love, and transitioning to the next phase of your life – whatever that may entail.

'You go from being the king of your domain – where you know exactly what your value is, what your job is, the influence you can have on your teammates. Then all of a sudden, you're standing on your own, in a room full of strangers, who are your new work friends. And they're wanting to talk to you about what you used to be, and all you want to focus on is what you want to become. And you're very unsure as to who you are.'

Cannon's experience – in losing his identity and sense of purpose at the point of retirement – is reminiscent of the phenomenon many new retirees encounter when they cease work. Major life transitions are hard. In an April 2017 interview with *The Sydney Morning Herald*'s Andrew Webster, champion racehorse trainer Gai Waterhouse communicated her own take on the psychological challenges of retirement, and the need to remain engaged in purposeful activity later in life.

She says, 'The saddest thing when people retire is that they become very unnecessary. When you are working, people need you. They have a reason to pick up the phone and ring you. When most men retire, suddenly nobody calls them. If you stop working ... nobody is going to call you. There's a reason for you to get up every day.'

Basketball superstar Lauren Jackson is another whose sporting career came to an abrupt end when her doctor told her she had 'no chance' of recovering from a serious knee injury. But she remained optimistic about her future, despite its uncertainties. In 2016, during a press conference at the Australian Institute of Sport to announce her retirement, Jackson said, 'To say goodbye to my love, what was my life, my identity ... You know it just hurts, it hurts a lot ... I feel kind of empty right now, but ready and excited for the next chapter – whatever that may be.'

Rightly or wrongly, for many people, their sense of self-worth is closely tied to their career or their business. The workplace is not just a source of remuneration. It is a forum for social connection, an environment of milestones achieved, and a significant source of meaning and personal validation. When a career comes to an end (sporting or otherwise), all of those things disappear – sometimes overnight – potentially leaving a void that makes the transition a major psychological challenge.

To prevent this from happening, your post-career life should be filled with meaningful commitments and activities. One athlete who has given plenty of thought to this issue is James Tomkins, OAM. James is an example of the importance of striving for balance through life's inevitable transitions.

A seven-time world champion rower, Tomkins competed in six Olympic Games between 1988 and 2008, winning gold medals in Barcelona, Atlanta and Athens, and bronze in Sydney. He was a member of the celebrated 'Oarsome Foursome' rowing team. He is currently National Sales Manager at UBS Global Asset Management and Chairman of the Australian Olympic Committee's Athletes' Commission.

While most of us will never know what it feels like to compete for our country at the highest level, there are parallels between an athlete's challenges of adjustment when a career ends, and the difficulties encountered by everyday retirees. Just as some athletes lose their sense of identity and self-worth when they retire, some 65-year-olds feel the same way; they believe their value is tied to their job title and the corporate knowledge and relationships they have built over decades. It can be hard to adjust from the buzz and energy of the workplace to everyday life at home.

Tomkins knows more than most about the challenges of shifting focus from the intensity and glory of competing on the world stage, to the relative calm of day-to-day life away from international competition. He was 45 when he formally announced his retirement from competitive rowing after making the decision not to continue training for the 2012 London Olympics. Tomkins felt that physically he could have continued training for the London games, but with a young family and multiple priorities, mentally he was not 100 per cent convinced he could commit to another gruelling training regimen after he had already achieved so much.

As we speak about what it feels like competing in world championships and Olympic Games, Tomkins reflects on European summers with his best friends, training and competing outdoors, the frequent media attention, and a team and support staff willing him on to perform and achieve new milestones. Living the dream.

But switching from that singular focus on training, performance and achievement at the highest level, to anything resembling a more normal existence is always going to present challenges.

'I remember coming home – coming back from a northern hemisphere summer,' he says. 'You get back to [Melbourne] Australia and you've been in this world, competing over in Europe with some of your best friends, having a really good time in an intense environment, and you go out on the footpath and take the dog for a walk, and it's dreary and cold and you think, "What the hell?" There's a big part of your life missing. Clearly others experience that as well and to a far greater degree.'

'A lot of athletes base their self-worth on results in sport, rather than on the challenge and the journey – which I think is far more important. Athletes put themselves out on a limb, and it is such a knife-edge of success or failure, result-wise. The fact is there is a huge amount of work in someone getting off their backside and trying to do something incredible. That's where the value is in the person – not whether they came first, second or third.'

Yet for two reasons, Tomkins was better prepared than many athletes to embark on a successful transition to life after sport. After studying Commerce and Economics at RMIT, Tomkins had already built a successful career in the financial services sector where he held senior roles at BT and (currently) UBS Global Asset Management – employers who have been supportive of his busy training and competition commitments.

His philosophy on the need to achieve balance also stood Tomkins in good stead for the next chapter of his life post-competition.

'A lot of athletes, when they transition, they've been involved in sports and had this single focus for a long period of time. I think it's really important to have significant physical goals still – whether it's doing a 200km bike ride, or a half-marathon, or a trek somewhere. Something to aim for physically. I try to have one of those a year or every couple of years that you actually aim for, so you've always got a goal that you're working towards – unrelated to what you previously did, but equally physically involved.'

Tomkins is a big believer in the importance of a balanced life. His pursuit of equilibrium was sparked early in his sporting career when he learned the story of the genesis of the Olympic Games in ancient Greece; in particular the cultural significance of non-sporting events that are part of the Olympic program.

'Two parts of Greece were at war with each other for so long they'd forgotten why they were actually fighting. So, they had a month-long competition. But it wasn't just athletics – there was philosophy and the arts was there as well. So, the Olympic Games was athletics for the body, philosophy for the mind and arts for the soul. In the modern Games, that's why you see the doves let loose, signifying peace and the reason for the Games. And in each city there will also be cultural programs and academic programs going hand-in-hand as acknowledgement of the importance of striving for balance in life. I heard about that and it made perfect sense for me because that's how I like to live – it's such a healthy way to think about life, touching those three areas,' he said.

It is often said that athletes retire twice. Once from their chosen field of endeavour, and again from the career they pursue away from the sporting arena. As our conversation turns to Tomkins' own retirement plans, he makes the point that while he has retired from competitive rowing, sport has been part of his DNA for as long as he can remember, and he intends to remain very active in a range of physical activities. Similarly, on the work front, he has no plans to retire completely at a particular point in time. Like many, he prefers the idea of ongoing involvement in a range of activities (paid and unpaid) for as long as opportunities exist. In addition to his role in the finance sector, Tomkins indicates he is likely to remain involved with various boards, charities and sports administration roles.

'I think, going forward, people won't necessarily retire from work. It will just be a dialling down or a modification of what they do over time, and I think that's really healthy. It depends what you're doing I guess, but you would see a lot of people retire and six months later they are just lost – they feel they don't have any relevance. There's no purpose. They might be fit and healthy when they're working, but as soon as they retire they fall in a heap. So I think while you may retire from what you're doing day to day, I think most people, especially most professional people, will stay active in some form or another. I think the value in someone with incredible experience over a long period of time should be tapped into as well.'

Life transitions can be hard at any age, and you can learn much from the major transitions of others. When seeking to retire well, the level of preparation and planning you undertake, and the support you access along the way, will have a major bearing on the results you achieve. The more consciously you have thought through life after work, the higher the probability you will thrive in the next stage – however that may look for you.

WORK, LEARN AND PLAY TILL YOU DROP

'It's time to start living the life you've imagined.'

HENRY JAMES

It is April 2017 and I'm sitting at a café in Sydney's Barrack Street speaking with Darren Wickham, an award-winning actuary, senior executive at TAL (a company specialising in life insurance), and an expert on the Australian super and retirement savings system.

In 2008, Wickham was named Australian Actuary of the Year after writing and presenting a report controversially titled 'It's time to abolish Retirement (and here's how to do it). Work, learn and play till you drop'. (At the time, he was working in the retirement division of wealth management company Mercer. He distinctly remembers a colleague suggesting that, given its title, the research may be a career-limiting move!)

At face value, the outright abolition of retirement sounds like an extreme position, but Wickham's report received a very positive reception from his peers, and many of the trends he identified in 2007 continue to play out before our eyes. Mature-age workforce participation has continued to steadily increase, healthy life expectancy has surged higher, and many older Australians are engaging in a gradual transition to retirement instead of a hard-and-fast ending to their career.

Some of Wickham's more notable arguments are that many people cannot afford a multi-decade retirement; that a fixed-aged retirement no longer makes sense in a world of rising life expectancies; and that, on average, people in their 60s are healthier than ever, so why encourage them to leave the workforce when they still have much to offer?

When it comes to the social and family considerations of retirement, he also wonders why we don't spread leisure more evenly over our lifetimes, rather than delaying a focus on leisure and recreation until age 65.

'I began thinking about this for purely selfish reasons,' he says. 'And I was thinking how can we afford 30 or 40 years of leisure in retirement, but we can't [afford] a four-day working week? Why don't we redistribute some of that leisure to earlier in our lives? The trade-off is we work a bit later, but we don't need as much savings.

'And it led me to explore the reasons why we have retirement. The main reason we have the institution of retirement is actually because of disability, and, to a lesser extent, unemployment. If you're disabled, you're cognitively impaired or you're physically impaired, then it is hard to participate in the workforce in the same way. Retirement is a dignified exit from the workforce.'

At the time of his research, Wickham noticed a recurring theme in many of his conversations with recent retirees. 'Because of the sense of purpose and meaning that work brought, and also the social interaction, a lot of people had substituted paid work for volunteer work. They were still capable of making a contribution, and they wanted to be involved in making a difference,' he says.

He agrees that employers need to retain the skills and experience of older workers, and that retirement as we know it does not suit the new, flexible world of work. Retirement also deprives people of the much-needed meaning and social connections derived from the workplace.

Central to Wickham's argument is the idea that while older Australians – who are capable of working – should be free to remain employed or retire, years of leisure should be funded from private savings, not subsidised by the federal government through social security benefits. (He acknowledges that appropriate support should always be provided to the disabled and the unemployed as needed.)

He highlights the work of author and Oxford University Professor of Gerontology, Sarah Harper, who traces the evolution of retirement from the late 1800s until the 21st century in her book, *Ageing Societies: Myths, Challenges and Opportunities*. Harper categorises the changing retirement landscape into the following periods:

- Pre-1890s: Work till you drop.

- 1890s–1950s: A rest before death.

- 1950s–1980s: Reward for hard work.

- 1980s–2000: Right to leisure.

- 2000 onwards: Phased retirement.

Wickham has a different view on the idea of 'phased retirement', commonly seen among older employees who transition from the rigours of full-time employment to part-time or contract work, which allows them to continue earning money without the same intensity.

'Phased retirement is not retirement,' he says. 'It is working flexibly at older ages. Arguably, this is no different to working flexibly at younger ages. The changes in the nature of work mean the same cycling in and out of the labour force will occur not only at older ages but at younger ages too,' he says.

One of Wickham's more radical proposals is the abolition of the Age Pension, replaced by a disability income payment at 25 per cent of average weekly earnings (payable for the duration of the disability) in the event an individual becomes disabled at any age.

'The difference between the proposed disability benefit and the current system of two separate benefits is that welfare payments would not be available for those capable of work,' he says.

Ten years since publishing his research, his views haven't changed.

'People are in much better health in their 60s and 70s than certainly my grandparents and their parents. We have this arbitrary 65 or 67 set-up – what's the significance of it? Today's 70-year-old is as healthy as a 50-year-old was 30 years ago. Most 70-year-olds are very capable of working ... And many are very willing if the opportunities are there,' he says.

Such is the mainstream relevance of the retirement age to the national conversation, Channel Nine's *60 Minutes* program recently revisited the issue with a segment called 'Work till you drop'. While the title is partly in keeping with Wickham's theories, it also brings back memories of the Labor Party's 2004 tongue-in-cheek description of then Federal Treasurer Peter Costello's proposed superannuation reforms, which were designed to encourage more older Australians to remain in the workforce – even if only on a part-time basis.

Back then, Costello reasoned that the ageing of the population was an inevitability, and policy makers really only had a limited number of options in reducing the economic fallout in a future with relatively fewer taxpayers and a ballooning number of Age Pension recipients.

In a February 2004 interview with the ABC's Kerry O'Brien on *The 7.30 Report*, he said, 'We are going to have an ageing demographic

… But the point I keep coming back to is this is a date with destiny – this cannot be changed. It was set in stone 30 years ago. It is going to work out over the next 40 years. The only choice we have is this: Do we start coming to grips with it early, in which case the adjustment will be less, or do we leave it so that the adjustment will be more drastic? I say we can address that demographic problem in four ways. You could increase tax – that's not something that is going to excite the public; you could restrict expenditures; you could run budget deficits and blow the problem out to future generations; or you can try and run the economy stronger and faster. That's what I think we have to aim at – a stronger economic performance.'

The Coalition's policy was about creating greater tax and workforce incentives to encourage mature-age workers to remain in employment for longer in order to stimulate the economy, broaden the tax base, and incrementally reduce welfare spending. Despite the apparent economic merits of the argument, critics of the policy sought to depict Costello as a heartless Treasurer promoting the idea of hard labour for Australia's elderly.

Fast-forward to July 2017, and Costello appears on *60 Minutes* in his capacity as Chairman of Nine Entertainment Company. He confirms his position – on the need for the Australian population to work longer – is little changed, and, if anything, the need for urgent action is growing. He says, 'We used to have five taxpayers for every person in retirement. Soon it's going to be two… The equation doesn't add up. It can't be done. I think there were people that thought at age 65, 67, 70, they might have enough to retire on. But they won't … And I would say to retirees now, you better take a big interest in this, because investment returns are going to be really challenged in the years ahead.

'[In the future] I don't think that there will be a concept of retirement. Retirement is a word from another age. The Rolling Stones are still singing rock in their 70s. As long as there are 80-year-old singers, 80-year-old rock-and-rollers will be turning out to listen to them.'

CONCLUSION

A NEW BEGINNING

'Do not go where the path may lead.
Go instead where there is no path and leave a trail.'

RALPH WALDO EMERSON

The conventional definition of retirement – work full-time until age 60 or 65, and then stop and spend your life at leisure – is completely outdated. It is a definition that is failing retirees who are increasingly unfulfilled by that experience, and it is failing a society that cannot afford to lose the skills, wisdom and taxes of an ageing population that is willing and able to continue making a contribution.

The end of the retirement age marks the beginning of a new era, which has the potential to achieve deeper meaning and fulfilment for individuals, and greater prosperity for society.

While longer life expectancies, government indebtedness, declining job security and financial complexity have combined to alter the retirement landscape irreversibly, this new reality has sown the seeds for a generation to completely re-engineer this phase of life in a way that is more rewarding for retirees, and beneficial for employers, government and future generations.

By reframing your attitude to the ageing population in positive terms, you can view this new era as an opportunity for personal growth. You may visualise a society that embraces the contribution of mature-age workers, and leverages the reality that this is the healthiest generation of Australians in their 50s, 60s and 70s in history.

If you're about to enter this phase of life, you will do so with a renewed sense of optimism. What was once a phase of life associated with 'endings' has evolved to be a time of new beginnings. A blank canvas providing the opportunity to re-engage with your purpose in life, and make conscious choices about how you will spend those extra years, gifted to us by rising living standards, medical advances, technological breakthroughs, and improvements in public education.

Health permitting, it is about treating this period as an opportunity to pursue and achieve all of those things you have yet to achieve – perhaps due to lack of time, lack of money, lack of imagination or fear. Living life to the fullest – whatever that looks like for you.

I am grateful to the inspiring individuals who shared their retirement experiences and insights for this book. Their stories demonstrate that the redefinition of retirement is well underway and that a better version is emerging.

We still have work to do to fully embrace the end of the retirement age, but there is much to be optimistic about.

The choice is yours.

40 REFLECTIONS ON RETIRING WELL

'It is never too late to be what you might have been.'

GEORGE ELIOT

I would like to leave you with some pearls of wisdom on planning a meaningful, purposeful and prosperous retirement.

And who better to ask than a group of people who have retired well in the last 10 years?

Without further ado, here are 40 hand-picked pieces of wisdom from recent retirees. I hope you find them useful.

1. 'Remember, you are retiring from paid employment – you are not retiring from life!'

2. 'Work on knowing who you are without your work identity, and move forward knowing that you are that same person the day after you retire.'

3. 'Start thinking about the different ways you can use all that you have learned and become to continue living a rich and full life as a retiree, and contribute to the lives of your family, friends and community.'

4. 'Having a positive mindset is paramount, along with faith in your ability to continue being a valued and contributing member of society.'

5. 'It's important to have financial security so that you can live comfortably, access all the services you need, and enjoy the pleasures of spending time with family and friends.'

6. 'You need to identify worthwhile purposes and passions to pursue, and not be afraid to make new starts.'

7. 'You need to find meaningful ways to contribute to your community – volunteer work is a great one. Find work that uses your skills or taps into your passions.'

8. 'Keep the mind and body active – everything else follows!'

9. 'Be absolutely debt free.'

10. 'It is a very enjoyable and satisfying phase – provided you have the financial plan in place for security, and a varied range of social activities and interaction.'

11. 'Set a financial plan that incorporates retirement and activities thereafter. Join groups. Be prepared for community work. Ensure social interaction. Keep abreast of local and global affairs, and ensure good family relationships exist with your spouse, children and grandchildren.'

12. 'Ensure that you do everything to protect your health.'

13. 'Get involved with a group of likeminded people who enjoy life and who are involved in "doing" things.'

14. 'Enjoy hobbies and interests, and be up with current world and domestic affairs.'

15. 'Sitting at home in a solo environment, with no outlet or activity, is a recipe for disaster.'

16. 'An old boss of mine once said that to keep your brain ticking, you need to speak to nine people a day. The number may be disputed but the communication side is paramount.'

17. 'I believe your journey to retirement starts around 40. It is at this stage you should have a reasonable idea of your final financial position. The goal should be to make this an eventuality.'

18. 'Long-term planning is a must.'

19. 'I have always liked the Nike logo – just do it.'

20. 'A happy life, whether one is retired or not, requires planning and structure that allows you to focus on the relationships and interests that are important to you.'

21. 'Given the constraints age and health may impose, it is even more important to focus on positive relationships and to maintain and/or develop interests outside that are sustaining and rewarding.'

22. 'Self-sufficiency, the ability to see beauty in your surroundings, and a sense of contentedness – together with a connection with your community – will enable a happy retirement.'

23. 'Retirement should not be a bookend of life but rather another stage. Maintaining an interest in current affairs and politics, and a flexible approach to new ideas and technology, is also important to one remaining in the mainstream of life, and not just parked in a fixed landscape of previously held beliefs and attitudes.'

24. 'Retirement is the opportunity to bring the wisdom you have obtained in your life into fruition for yourself and others.'

25. 'I see full-time retirement as an opportunity to travel more and to undertake community work.'

26. 'Live as if you had an unlimited life expectancy.'

27. 'Retirement is the third stage of life when you have the freedom to indulge yourself.'

28. 'Plan early for sufficient funds to live comfortably.'

29. 'Don't sit back and wait to be amused. Get out and find interests – things you've always wanted to do but not had the time.'

30. 'Having a husband around "full-time" was quite a challenge – all of a sudden you have to check out and check in.'

31. 'Plan early, and, once you have that lump sum, get good advice and don't just put it in the bank.'

32. 'I do voluntary work to stimulate me – babysitting, and volunteering at our local art gallery. Both are quite demanding!'

33. 'Retire when you are still healthy and can enjoy it.'

34. 'Get good financial advice. Think through what sort of things you want to do in your older years. Prioritise and have a plan for when and what you want to do. Don't be complacent.'

35. 'It's important to be able to afford to eat good food and maintain good physical health.'

36. 'Essential inputs are friends, being happy with where you live, accessing local cultural and fun activities, exercising, and appreciating nature and beauty.'

37. 'I have found great fulfillment in assisting my daughter and her husband with daily chores and the care of their first baby. Ultimately, I want to fill some time by doing voluntary work with a service organisation like the Salvos or St Vincent de Paul.'

38. 'Hobbies or interests are essential. That is the strongest recommendation I would put to anybody.'

39. 'I now know that retirement is not about preparing for the end. It is about making new beginnings, setting ourselves challenges, and accomplishing amazing goals.'

40. 'I think primarily you need to be occupied and do something you enjoy doing. Find something that really interests you ... It might be studying law, it might be making wooden tables, it might be painting, or something with your hands. Everybody's different, but I think a crucial element is to have something that interests you, that can occupy you, and give you some satisfaction. You've got to have something to look forward to.'

ACKNOWLEDGEMENTS

Nearly four years ago, I opened a blank notepad and scribbled the first words of this book. I recall sitting on a sundrenched balcony in the Blue Mountains township of Leura – oblivious to the sacrifices and time commitment of the journey ahead.

I owe a debt of gratitude to countless people who have since been generous enough to provide their valuable time, experience, stories and insights to bring this project to life. In an undertaking of this size, momentum is everything, and I thank each and every one of you for propelling me towards the creation of this book.

Thank you to Jacqui Pretty for lighting the pathway and providing the structure, guidance and encouragement to convert a disparate collection of ideas into a meaningful narrative. Thank you for working with me to create order out of chaos.

It was a privilege to work with editor Michelle Hammond, who knows when to rein me in and when to let me go. Thank you for weaving your magic, and thank you for your patience, honesty and good humour.

I was fortunate enough to meet Jon Glass while researching this book, and I was immediately taken by his energy, passion and wise counsel. Thank you for so many invaluable contributions to the research effort and thank you for believing in the importance of this work.

I have long admired Dr Tim Sharp (Dr Happy) from afar, and I was thrilled to have the opportunity to interview him about the pursuit of meaning and purpose as we age. I am in awe of the work that you do. Thank you for your encouragement and generosity of spirit.

James Tomkins, OAM, thank you for a fascinating conversation and for offering profound insights into life transitions that are relevant to all generations. With one story, you transformed my thinking on achieving balance in life and for that I am grateful. *Athletics for the body, philosophy for the mind, art for the soul.*

Darren Wickham's prescient 2007 research paper foreshadowed many retirement trends that have since come to pass. Thank you for taking the time to share your latest thinking on retirement issues, and thank you for your support and encouragement.

Rebecca Wilson, CEO of Starts at 60, is a powerhouse of energy and ideas. Thank you for your time and support. Your passion and advocacy for older Australians is inspiring.

Thank you to Valerie Khoo, CEO of the Australian Writers' Centre. The feedback you provided on a feature article I wrote in 2007 inspired me to (eventually) devote more time to writing. This book is the result.

Dr Ruth Williams was a joy to interview. I am in awe of your passion and advocacy for the valuable role older Australians can play in society, if they are just given the opportunities to contribute. Thank you for being generous with your time and for sharing your expertise and enthusiasm.

I am grateful to Ian and Wendy Thompson for sharing such detailed insights and stories of your own retirement transition. Kate and I cherish your friendship and the wisdom and encouragement you so willingly provide.

Ross and Bev Homel's enthusiasm for this project was highly motivating. Thank you for taking the time to contribute your experiences and insights. I learn so much from every conversation with you both.

Thanks also to Bernard Salt, Graham Rich, Simon Russell, Fiona McLean, Scott Hirst, Dr Merryn Dawborn-Gundlach, Dr Max Roser, Judy and Shane Higgins, Andy Ross, Trish and Tony Hartley, Margaret-Anne and Wayne Hayes, John and Sandra, Bruce and Patricia Chanter, Vin and Lynne De Celis, Steve and Liz Watts, Christine and Anthony Melican, and Jon and Cecilia Kramar.

My outstanding Practice Manager, Stacey Brown, keeps me organised, fuelled and focused. Thank you for your optimism and belief.

To my mum Jenny, thank you for your invaluable advice and input into this project and for your unconditional love and support. You inspire more people than you know, and I am so proud to be your son.

To my dad Kerry, I am in awe of your work ethic, and your ability to research and publish books at such a prolific rate. You make it look effortless. Thank you for instilling in me the idea that 'it is by taking chances that we succeed.'

To my three beautiful children – Rose, Fletcher and Samuel. You fill my heart with so much joy, and words cannot express the pride I feel to be your dad. More often than you may ever realise, at 1am, while you are fast asleep and I am writing, you are my inspiration to keep going – you are my *Ikigai*. My challenge to you, as you grow up, is to find what it is you love to do – that which you are truly passionate about. When you find it, you will know, because it will be the last thing you think about before falling asleep and the first thing on your mind when you wake up. There is no rush, but when you work it out, make a conscious choice to build your life around those activities (and people) that truly light you up. Always follow your heart, and stay kind, curious and caring. The world needs more people like you.

Lastly, I will be forever grateful to my beautiful wife, Kate, for backing me to bring this book to life. Thank you for your energy, patience, love and support. Thank you for momentum. Thank you for confidence. Thank you for simultaneously believing in me and challenging me to raise the bar. Thank you for tolerating the chaos of a dining table covered in manila folders and mountains of research for weeks on end. Thank you for entertaining our kids when I had a deadline looming. Thank you for juggling a successful corporate career and a growing business, while always finding time to put a smile on the faces of our three treasures. You inspire me, and it is a privilege to walk beside you as we follow our dreams.

ABOUT THE AUTHOR

David Kennedy is an author, consultant, and retirement planning expert. He is the owner of Hillross Pacific Advisory, an award-winning wealth advisory firm based in Sydney.

In 2014 he received the *Hillross Adviser of the Year* award, and his views on retirement trends have featured in *The Australian*, *AFR Asset* and *Financial Planning* magazine.

David has extensive experience in the wealth management industry with previous roles in corporate strategy and business consulting. He is a practitioner at Kaplan Professional (a leading national provider of education and training in financial services), and a proud partner of the Cancer Council Pro Bono Program.

He lives in Sydney with his wife and three children.

END NOTES

INTRODUCTION

Harper, Sarah. 'Reformations 10: Ageing' Lecture, Hay Festival, Wales, Hay-on-Wye, 29 May, 2017. Retrieved from https://www.hayfestival.com/p-12205-sarah-harper.aspx

Friedman, Thomas L. *Thank you for being late: An optimist's guide to thriving in the age of accelerations*, 1st edn. New York. Farrar, Straus and Giroux, 2016.

Australian Bureau of Statistics, 2014, 18 September, *Australian Historical Population Statistics*. 3105.0.65.001. Retrieved from http://www.abs.gov.au/ausstats/abs@.nsf/mf/3105.0.65.001

Australian Bureau of Statistics, 1988, 1 January, *History of Pensions and Other Benefits in Australia. 1301.0 Year Book Australia, 1988*. Retrieved from http://www.abs.gov.au/AUSSTATS/abs@.nsf/3d68c56307742d8fca257090002029cd/8e72c4526a94aaedca2569de00296978!OpenDocument

Australian Institute of Health and Welfare. *Trends in life expectancy*. Retrieved from http://www.aihw.gov.au/deaths/life-expectancy/#trends

Irvine, Jessica. 'With an ageing population should you reconsider your retirement plans?' *The Daily Telegraph*, 26 November, 2013. Retrieved from http://www.dailytelegraph.com.au/business/jessica-irvine/with-an-ageing-population-should-you-reconsider-your-retirement-plans/news-story/a82516fc6a435351472b112796e4c0a3

Keating, Paul. 'Commonwealth insurance scheme needed for 80-100 year-olds,' Interview by Tony Jones. *Lateline*, Australian Broadcasting Corporation, 8 May 2014. Retrieved from http://www.abc.net.au/lateline/content/2014/s4001033.htm

Goh, Jassmyn. 'Super needs to be reconceptualised' *Super Review*, 2 February 2017. Retrieved from http://www.superreview.com.au/news/superannuation/super-needs-be-reconceptualised

Fahy, Martin, Dr. 'Superannuation in 2017: what does good look like?' Speech, Pritchitt Partners Annual New Year Function, 31 January 2017, Sydney. Transcript retrieved from https://cuffelinks.com.au/stop-policy-tinkering-bring-ideas

Salt, Bernard. 'Ageing Australia: Pluses and minuses for a nation showing its age.' *The Australian*, 11 August 2016 Retrieved from http://www.theaustralian.com.au/business/opinion/bernard-salt-demographer/ageing-australia-pluses-and-minuses-for-nation-showing-its-age/news-story/9b201db915fa3acc21dc9a18585e4810

Costello, Peter. 'Treasurer Budget Lock-up Press Conference.' Transcript, Canberra, 11 May, 2004. Retrieved from http://www.petercostello.com.au/transcripts/2004/2768-budget-budget-lock-up-press-conference-parliament-house-canberra

Costello, Peter. 'Work till You Drop.' Interview by Charles Wooley. *60 Minutes*, The Nine Network, 2 July 2017.

Australian Bureau of Statistics, 2015, 29 October, Births, Australia, 2014. 3301.0. Retrieved from http://www.abs.gov.au/ausstats/abs@.nsf/Previousproducts/3301.0Main%20Features42014?opendocument&tabname=Summary&prodno=3301.0&issue=2014&num=&view=

Roy Morgan Research. 'Age of intending retirees increasing due to changes in pension eligibility, superannuation rules and economic uncertainty.' Media release, 18 January, 2017. Retrieved from http://www.roymorgan.com/findings/7106-age-of-intending-retirees-increasing-in-australia-201701181109

Deloitte Access Economics. 'Increasing participation among older workers: the grey army advances.' [Report prepared for the Australian Human Rights Commission], 2012. Retrieved from https://www2.deloitte.com/au/en/pages/economics/articles/increasing-participation-among-older-workers.html

Collier, Grace. 'Industrial Relations and Respectful Relationships'. *Q&A*, Australian Broadcasting Corporation, 17 October, 2016.

Rich, Graham. 'Backgrounder: The long and short of it.' Portfolio Construction Forum, *19 August, 2016*.

Mitchell, Harold. 'Equity is good, but cash is king in retirement.' *The Sydney Morning Herald*, 21 April, 2017. Retrieved from http://www.smh.com.au/business/banking-and-finance/equity-is-good-but-cash-is-king-in-retirement-20170420-gvok9w.html

Honoré, Carl. *In praise of slow: How a worldwide movement is challenging the cult of speed*. Toronto: Vintage Canada, 2004.

Honoré, Carl. *Carl Honoré: In praise of slowness [video file]*. July, 2005. Retrieved from https://www.ted.com/talks/carl_honore_praises_slowness

PART ONE

Human Longevity, Inc. 'Human Longevity Inc. (HLI) launched to promote healthy aging using advances in genomics and stem cell therapies.' Media release, 4 March 2014. Retrieved from http://www.humanlongevity.com/human-longevity-inc-hli-launched-to-promote-healthy-aging-using-advances-in-genomics-and-stem-cell-therapies/

Diamandis, Peter. *Peter Diamandis: Imagining the Future: The Transformation of Humanity* [video file]. December, 2016. Retrieved from https://www.youtube.com/watch?v=7XrbzlR9QmI

Kontis, Vasilis, Bennett, James E, Mathers, Colin D, Li, Guangquan, Foreman, Kyle, and Ezzati, Majid. 'Future life expectancy in 35 industrialised countries: projections with a Bayesian model ensemble.' *The Lancet*, Volume 389 (Number 10076), 1323-1335. http://dx.doi.org/10.1016/S0140-6736(16)32381-9

Australian Bureau of Statistics. 'Life expectancy hits a new high.' Media release, 27 October, 2016. Retrieved from http://www.abs.gov.au/ausstats/abs@.nsf/lookup/3302.0.55.001Media%20Release12013-2015

Magellan Asset Management Limited. Annual Investor Report: Magellan Global, June 2016.

Douglass, Hamish. 'Are we there yet?' Magellan National Adviser Briefing. Sydney, 14 September, 2016.

Sinclair, David. *David Sinclair: A Cure for Ageing?* [video file]. May, 2013. Retrieved from https://tedxsydney.com/talk/a-cure-for-ageing/

Aging Reversed. 'David Sinclair – Slowing down aging' [video file]. 17 July, 2016. Retrieved from https://www.youtube.com/watch?v=lA4DbN01q70

Zubrzycki, John. 'Never say die: David Sinclair's anti-ageing quest.' *The Sydney Morning Herald*, 3 October 2015. Retrieved from http://www.smh.com.au/good-weekend/never-say-die-david-sinclairs-antiageing-quest-20150916-gjocnm.html

Macdonald, Fiona. 'It's Happening: Scientists Can Now Reverse DNA Ageing in Mice.' *Science Alert*, 25 March, 2017. Retrieved from https://www.sciencealert.com/scientists-have-successfully-reversed-dna-ageing-in-mice

Strange, Adario. 'Microsoft CEO: Apple iPhone will fail.' *Wired,* 2 May, 2007. Retrieved from https://www.wired.com/2007/05/microsoft_ceo_a/

University of California – San Diego. 'Nanoengineers 3-D print biomimetic blood vessel networks.' *Science Daily*, 2 March 2017. Retrieved from www.sciencedaily.com/releases/2017/03/170302133430.htm

Woolf, Martin. 'An interview with Dr Joseph Murray, Organ Transplant Pioneer.' *On the Beat,* 25 May, 2014. Retrieved from http://www.liveonny.org/uploaded_files/tinymce/files/interview_joseph_murray.pdf

Commonwealth of Australia. *Intergenerational Report 2015 – Australia in 2055*. Commonwealth of Australia, Canberra, 2015. Retrieved from http://www.treasury.gov.au/PublicationsAndMedia/Publications/2015/2015-Intergenerational-Report

Lynch, Kevin. 'World's oldest person Emma Morano dies aged 117.' *Guinness World Records,* 17 April, 2017. Retrieved from http://www.guinnessworldrecords.com/news/2017/4/worlds-oldest-person-emma-morano-dies-aged-117-469018

Povoledo, Elisabetta. 'Raw eggs and no husband since '38 keep her young at 115.' *The New York Times*, 14 February, 2015. Retrieved from https://www.nytimes.com/2015/02/15/world/raw-eggs-and-no-husband-since-38-keep-her-young-at-115.html

Bieber, Nicholas, and Dougall, Sabrina. 'Revealed: Oldest woman in the world says EGGS are the secret to long life.' *Daily Star*, 16 April 2017. Retrieved from http://www.dailystar.co.uk/news/latest-news/605933/Emma-Morano-oldest-person-in-world-dies-last-survivor-born-19th-Century

Suzuki, Makoto, Willcox, Bradley, and Willcox, Craig. *The Okinawa Centenarian Study*. Retrieved from http://www.okicent.org/index.html

Suzuki, Makoto, Willcox, Bradley, and Willcox, Craig. *The Okinawa Program: How the World's Longest-Lived People Achieve Everlasting Health – and How You Can Too*. New York, Three Rivers Press, 2002.

Buettner, Dan. *Dan Buettner: How to live to be 100+* [video file]. September, 2009. Retrieved from https://www.ted.com/talks/dan_buettner_how_to_live_to_be_100

Stephens, Scott and Williams, Lisa A. 'Why Milestones Matter: Time, Social Meaning and the Measure of the Moral Life.' *ABC Religion and Ethics*. Australian Broadcasting Corporation, 10 May, 2017. Retrieved from http://www.abc.net.au/religion/articles/2017/05/19/4672168.htm

PART TWO

HSBC. *The Future of Retirement: Shifting Sands* [Global Report], 2017. Retrieved from www.hsbc.com/-/media/hsbc.../170426-the-future-of-retirement-shifting-sands.pdf

Shepherd, Tony. 'Are the baby boomers the greediest generation ever? *The Sydney Morning Herald*, 22 May 2016. Retrieved from http://www.smh.com.au/comment/are-the-baby-boomers-the-greediest-generation-ever-20160520-gp0c17.html

The Association of Superannuation Funds of Australia. *ASFA Retirement Standard*, March, 2017. Retrieved from https://www.superannuation.asn.au/resources/retirement-standard

Meers, Daniel. 'Federal Cabinet Reshuffle: Scott Morrison picks up Social Services portfolio in bid to stop the bludgers.' *The Daily Telegraph,* 21 December, 2014. Retrieved from http://www.dailytelegraph.com.au/news/nsw/federal-cabinet-reshuffle-scott-morrison-picks-up-social-services-portfolio-in-bid-to-stop-the-bludgers/news-story/da5ed05baee885d7e4613eec0bc91222

Crowe, David. 'More cuts needed to fund new DSP programs, says Scott Morrison.' *The Weekend Australian,* 3 November, 2015. Retrieved from http://www.theaustralian.com.au/national-affairs/health/more-cuts-needed-to-fund-new-dsp-programs-says-scott-morrison/news-story/afa0fbedb3e0c47c43dd234fd7a04a12

Credlin, Peta. 'Peta Credlin on how welfare dependence is ruining our economy.' *Herald Sun,* 29 October 2016. Retrieved from http://www.heraldsun.com.au/news/opinion/peta-credlin-on-how-welfare-dependence-is-ruining-our-economy/news-story/f6120b0933e12e597deb462c0da164ba

Bragg, Andrew. 'Welfare for millionaires: unions defend the indefensible.' *Australian Financial Review,* 3 January 2017. Retrieved from http://www.afr.com/news/policy/welfare-for-millionaires-unions-defend-the-indefensible-20170103-gtl5iw

Hockey, Joe. 'The end of the age of entitlement.' Address to the Institute of Economic Affairs, London, 17 April, 2012.

Bramston, Troy. 'Federal election 2016: reformers knew how to sell policy.' *The Australian,* 17 May 2016. Retrieved from http://www.theaustralian.com.au/opinion/columnists/troy-bramston/federal-election-2016-reformers-knew-how-to-sell-policy/news-story/47681b295f19ec252dd59d8820cc4941

Colebatch, Tim. 'We simply can't have our cake and eat it too.' *The Age,* 26 November, 2013. Retrieved from http://www.smh.com.au/comment/we-simply-cant-have-our-cake-and-eat-it-too-20131125-2y5wg.html

Jericho, Greg. 'Hockey the fantasy economist may as well have farewelled Middle-Earth.' *The Guardian,* 22 October, 2015. Retrieved from https://www.theguardian.com/business/grogonomics/2015/oct/22/hockey-the-fantasy-economist-may-as-well-have-farewelled-middle-earth

Greenwood, Ross. 'Money Minute: A dose of reality'. *Today Show,* The Nine Network, 5 April, 2017.

Greenwood, Ross. *Ray Hadley Morning Show* [radio broadcast], Macquarie Radio Network, 5 April 2017.

Frischmann, Brett M. 'Some Thoughts on Shortsightedness and Intergenerational Equity.' *Loyola University Chicago Law Journal*, Vol. 36, 10 May, 2005. Retrieved from SSRN: https://ssrn.com/abstract=721025

Westal, Andrea. 'An Opportunity for Transformational Change: A Provocation on the Potential for a Future Generations Commissioner for the UK.' Foundation for Democracy and Sustainable Development, July 2017. Retrieved from http://www.fdsd.org/publications/aw_opportunity-transformational-change/

PART THREE

Australian Institute of Health and Welfare. *Employment and economic participation – work and retirement.* Canberra: AIHW, 2016. Retrieved from http://www.aihw. gov.au/ageing/older-australia-at-a-glance/engagement/employment-and-economic/

Bersin, Josh. 'Why IBM Acquired Kenexa.' *Forbes*, 27 August, 2012. Retrieved from https://www.forbes.com/sites/joshbersin/2012/08/27/why-ibm-acquired-kenexa/#5bdc11951372

Karsan, Rudy. *Rudy Karsan: How the future of work is not 'jobs'* [Video file]. May, 2016. Retrieved from https://www.tedxcalgary.ca/talks/how-future-work-not-jobs

Clifford, Catherine. 'Apple CEO Tim Cook: Don't work for money … you will never be happy'. *CNBC Make It,* 9 February 2017. Retrieved from https://www.cnbc com/2017/02/09/apple-ceo-tim-cook-dont-work-for-money-you-will-never-be-happy.html

Gates, Bill. 'Millenium 2000: Bill Gates Discusses Microsoft, Philanthropy and the Future of Computers' [television broadcast]. *Larry King Live Weekend,* 1 January, 2000. Retrieved from http://transcripts.cnn.com/TRANSCRIPTS/0001/01/lklw.00.html

Brighton-Hall, Rhonda, and Cassells, Rebecca. *Happy workers: How satisfied are Australians at work?* Curtin University and mwah, April, 2017. Retrieved from http://bcec.edu.au/publications/happy-workers-how-satisfied-are-australians-at-work/

Pocock, Barbara. 'Meaningful Work in the 21st Century: What makes good jobs good, and what gives them their occasional dark sides.' Foenander Public Lecture. The University of Melbourne, 21 October, 2009. Retrieved from http://fbe.unimelb. edu.au/__data/assets/pdf_file/0020/661502/Foenander_24th_2009.pdf

Australian Institute of Health and Welfare. *Australia's welfare 2015.* Australia's welfare no. 12. Cat. No. AUS 189. Canberra: AIHW, 2015.

Ong, Rachel, Wood, Gavin, Atalay, Kadir and Cigdem-Bayram, Melek 'Australians are working longer so they can pay off their mortgage debt.' *The Conversation,* 29 June, 2017. Retrieved from https://theconversation.com/australians-are-working-longer-so-they-can-pay-off-their-mortgage-debt-79578

Commonwealth of Australia *Intergenerational Report 2015 - Australia in 2055*. Commonwealth of Australia, Canberra, 2015. Retrieved from http://www.treasury. gov.au/PublicationsAndMedia/Publications/2015/2015-Intergenerational-Report

Gartrell, Adam. 'Government jobs program falls 95 per cent short of target.' *The Sydney Morning Herald*, 8 November, 2015. Retrieved from http://www.smh.com. au/federal-politics/political-news/government-jobs-program-falls-95-per-cent-short-of-target-20151107-gkt8pn.html

Australian Human Rights Commission. *Willing to work: National Inquiry into Employment Discrimination Against Older Australians and Australians with Disability*, 2016. Retrieved from https://www.humanrights.gov.au/sites/default/files/ document/publication/WTW_2016_Full_Report_AHRC_ac.pdf

Brice, Jenny. 'In the modern workplace, age 50 is considered old.' *The Sydney Morning Herald*, 2 March, 2016. Retrieved from http://www.smh.com.au/comment/time-to-rectify-costly-age-discrimination-in-the-workforce-20160301-gn73jq.html

Williams, Ruth. 'Seniorpreneur: We need you.' *Pursuit*, 30 March, 2016. Retrieved from https://pursuit.unimelb.edu.au/articles/seniorpreneur-we-need-you

Pash, Chris. 'An inside look at the tool employers will soon use to check your social media profile.' *Business Insider Australia*, 30 August, 2016. Retrieved from https:// www.businessinsider.com.au/an-inside-look-at-the-tool-employers-will-soon-use-to-check-your-social-media-profile-2016-8

PART FOUR

Keating, Paul. 'Commonwealth insurance scheme needed for 80-100 year-olds.' Interview by Tony Jones. *Lateline*. Australian Broadcasting Corporation, 8 May, 2014. Retrieved from http://www.abc.net.au/lateline/content/2014/s4001033.htm

Deloitte. *Adequacy and the Australian Superannuation System: A Deloitte Point of View 2014*, June, 2014.

Australian Institute of Health and Welfare. *Australia's welfare 2015*. Australia's welfare no. 12. Cat. No. AUS 189. Canberra: AIHW, 2015.

Australian Unity. 'Government super changes are here, but majority are unprepared' Media release, 19 July, 2017. Retrieved from https://www.australianunity.com.au/media-centre/news-and-media/government-super-changes-are-here-but-majority-unprepared

Empirica Research. *Retirement Planning Research.* [Research report prepared for Australian Unity] May, 2017. Retrieved from https://www.australianunity.com.au/wealth/~/media/publicsite/documents/retirement%20planning%20survey%202017/retirement-report-20170704.ashx

National Australia Bank Limited. *Special Report: MLC Retirement Survey Q1 2014.* Retrieved from https://www.mlc.com.au/content/dam/mlc/documents/pdf/media-centre/media_releases_mlc_retirement_survey.pdf

Elsworth, Sophie. 'The dream expectations in retirement cost more than Australians think.' *News Corp Australia Network*, 22 December, 2013. Retrieved from http://www.news.com.au/finance/superannuation/the-dream-expectations-in-retirement-cost-more-than-australians-think/news-story/d7435ae7a2327bfc21019d9c93e2c2b8

The Association of Superannuation Funds of Australia. *ASFA Retirement Standard,* March, 2017. Retrieved from https://www.superannuation.asn.au/resources/retirement-standard

Russell, Simon. *Applying Behavioural Finance in Australia: 12 Strategies for Fund Managers, Financial Advisers, Asset Consultants, Super Funds & Other Sophisticated Investors.* Sydney. Publicious Pty Ltd, 2016.

Jordan, Philippe. *This time is not different, we're just predisposed to think so* [Presentation]. PortfolioConstruction Forum Conference – The long and short of it. Sydney, 24 August, 2016.

HSBC. *The Future of Retirement: Shifting Sands* [Global Report], 2017. Retrieved from www.hsbc.com/-/media/hsbc.../170426-the-future-of-retirement-shifting-sands.pdf

HSBC. *The Future of Retirement: Life After Work* [Global Report], 2013. Retrieved from https://www.hsbc.com.vn/1/PA_ES_Content_Mgmt/content/vietnam/personal/financial_planning/document/life-after-work.pdf

Matthews, Gail. *The Effectiveness of Four Coaching Techniques in Enhancing Goal Achievement: Writing Goals, Formulating Action Steps, Making a Commitment, and Accountability.* 9th Annual International Conference on Psychology. Athens, Greece, 25-28 May, 2015. Findings retrieved from http://www.dominican.edu/academics/ahss/undergraduate-programs/psych/faculty/assets-gail-matthews/research-summary2.pdf

Klapdor, Michael. *Pensions: Budget Review 2015-16.* Parliament of Australia. Canberra, May, 2015. Retrieved from http://www.aph.gov.au/About_Parliament/Parliamentary_Departments/Parliamentary_Library/pubs/rp/BudgetReview201516/Pensions

The Association of Superannuation Funds of Australia. *ASFA Retirement Standard*, March 2017. Retrieved from https://www.superannuation.asn.au/resources/retirement-standard

Thornhill, Peter. *Motivated Money: You've Invested Well? Compared to What?* Melbourne. Peter Thornhill, 2002.

Fitzsimmons, Caitlin. 'Millennials are better with money that I was in my 20s.' *The Sydney Morning Herald*, 25 June, 2017. Retrieved from http://www.smh.com.au/money/investing/millennials-are-better-with-money-than-i-was-in-my-20s-20170623-gwxjsh.html

PART FIVE

Cruz, Cassia. 'Should you Market to Baby Boomers on Social Media?' [blog post]. *Social Media Marketing Institute*, 18 February, 2017. Retrieved from http://www.smminstitute.com.au/blog-view/should-you-market-to-baby-boomers-on-social-media-32

Sensis Pty Ltd. *Sensis Social Media Report 2017: Chapter 1 – Australians and Social Media,* 22 June, 2017. Retrieved from https://www.sensis.com.au/asset/PDFdirectory/Sensis-Social-Media-Report-2017.pdf

Swayme, Matt. 'Sorry kids, seniors want to connect and communicate on Facebook, too.' *Penn State News*, 12 April, 2016. Retrieved from http://news.psu.edu/story/403464/2016/04/12/research/sorry-kids-seniors-want-connect-and-communicate-facebook-too

Wilson, Rebecca. 'Life starts at 60.' Interview by Wendy Kingston, *Weekend Today*, The Nine Network, 8 March, 2015. Retrieved from https://www.youtube.com/watch?v=ManE4L2fmlE

Hurley, Ben. 'Engaged at 60: new blog StartsAtSixty.com.au finds a big audience hungry for seniors-friendly social media.' *Australian Financial Review*, 24 October, 2013. Retrieved from http://www.afr.com/leadership/entrepreneur/engaged-at-60-new-blog-startsatsixtycom-finds-a-big-audience-hungry-for-seniorsfriendly-social-media-20131024-jz2o8

Seven West Media. '*Seven West Media confirms investment in Starts at 60.*' Media release, 16 February, 2016. Retrieved from http://www.sevenwestmedia.com.au/docs/default-source/business-unit-news/seven-west-media-confirms-investment-in-starts-at-60.pdf?sfvrsn=2

Australian Ageing Agenda. 'Loneliness leading concern for older people.' *Australian Ageing Agenda*, 12 September, 2013. Retrieved from http://www.australianageingagenda.com.au/2013/09/12/loneliness-leading-concern-for-older-people/

Holland, Caroline and Minocha, Shailey. 'For older people, beating loneliness isn't just about where and who they live with.' *The Conversation*, 24 August, 2015. Retrieved from https://theconversation.com/for-older-people-beating-loneliness-isnt-just-about-where-and-who-they-live-with-46308

National Seniors Australia. 'Seniors travelling more, report shows.' [Blog post]. National Seniors Australia, 17 March, 2016. Retrieved from https://nationalseniors.com.au/be-informed/news-articles/seniors-travelling-more-report-shows

World Tourism Organisation (UNWTO). 'Sustained growth in international tourism despite challenges.' *UNWTO World Tourism Barometer*, Volume 15 [Advance release], January, 2017. Retrieved from http://cf.cdn.unwto.org/sites/all/files/pdf/unwto_barom17_01_january_excerpt_.pdf

Hosie, Rachel. 'Paris Tourist Numbers Drop Due to Fears Over Further Terror Attacks.' *The Independent*, 22 February, 2017. Retrieved from http://www.independent.co.uk/travel/paris-tourist-numbers-drop-franch-terror-attacks-further-charlie-hebdo-bataclan-shooting-isis-a7592836.html

Ruddock, Philip. Commonwealth of Australia: *Parliamentary Debates. House of Representatives – Statements by Members*. Speech, Canberra, 4 June, 2015. Retrieved from http://parlinfo.aph.gov.au/parlInfo/genpdf/chamber/hansardr/494c836a-e9b4-4f50-9c2b-57185780ab51/0074/hansard_frag.pdf;fileType=application%2Fpdf

Australian Institute of Health and Welfare (AIHW). *Australian Cancer Incidence and Mortality books: Ovarian cancer*. Canberra: AIHW, 2016. http://www.aihw.gov.au/acim-books

Cancer Council Australia. *Ovarian Cancer*, 13 April, 2017. Retrieved from http://www.cancer.org.au/about-cancer/types-of-cancer/ovarian-cancer.html

PART SIX

Sharp, Tim. *Live Happier, Live Longer: Your guide to positive ageing and making the most of life*. Sydney. Allen & Unwin, 2014.

Ferguson, Sarah. 'After the Game: Elite athletes blow the whistle on the high price paid for sporting glory' *Four Corners*. Australian Broadcasting Corporation, 1 May, 2017. Retrieved from http://www.abc.net.au/4corners/stories/2017/05/01/4659870.htm

Wickham, Darren. *It's time to abolish Retirement (and here's how to do it) – Work, learn and play till you drop*. Institute of Actuaries of Australia – Biennial Convention, Christchurch, 23-26 September 2007. Retrieved from http://www.feal.asn.au/wp-content/uploads/2015/12/Wickham_Its-time-to-abolish-retirement.pdf

Harper, Sarah. *Ageing Societies: Myths, challenges and opportunities*. London. Hodder Arnold, 2006.

Costello, Peter. 'Costello tackles workforce dilemma.' Interview with Kerry O'Brien, *7.30 Report*. Australian Broadcasting Corporation, 25 February, 2004. Retrieved from http://www.abc.net.au/7.30/content/2004/s1053375.htm

Costello, Peter. 'Work till You Drop.' Interview by Charles Wooley. *60 Minutes*, The Nine Network, 2 July 2017.

www.ingramcontent.com/pod-product-compliance
Lightning Source LLC
Chambersburg PA
CBHW060238220326
41598CB00027B/3972